Wine in Ancient Egypt

A cultural and analytical study

Maria Rosa Guasch Jané

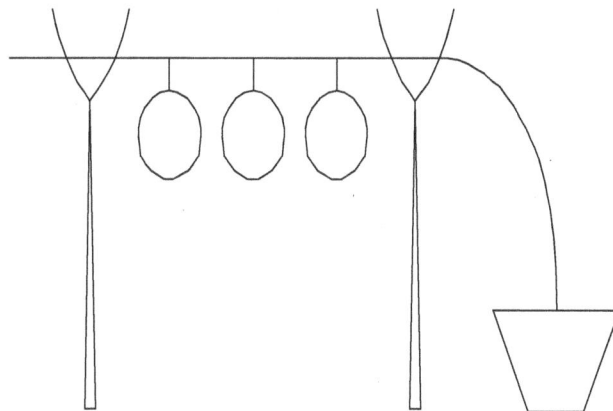

BAR International Series 1851
2008

Published in 2016 by
BAR Publishing, Oxford

BAR International Series 1851

Wine in Ancient Egypt

ISBN 978 1 4073 0338 3

BAR Publishing is the trading name of British Archaeological Reports (Oxford) Ltd.
British Archaeological Reports was first incorporated in 1974 to publish the BAR
Series, International and British. In 1992 Hadrian Books Ltd became part of the BAR
group. This volume was originally published by Archaeopress in conjunction with
British Archaeological Reports (Oxford) Ltd / Hadrian Books Ltd, the Series principal
publisher, in 2008. This present volume is published by BAR Publishing, 2016.

Printed in England

BAR
PUBLISHING

BAR titles are available from:

BAR Publishing
122 Banbury Rd, Oxford, OX2 7BP, UK
EMAIL info@barpublishing.com
PHONE +44 (0)1865 310431
FAX +44 (0)1865 316916
www.barpublishing.com

AUTHOR'S NOTE

The present monograph is based on my doctoral dissertation presented to the Department of Nutrition and Food Science, Faculty of Pharmacy, at the University of Barcelona.

The idea arised long time ago, after noticing that no thorough investigation of Egyptian wine residue samples has been done.

This project, "Wine in ancient Egypt", was financially supported by Codorníu SA winery and the Spanish Foundation for Wine Culture.

The publication of this book would not have been possible without the help and encouragement of my friends Montse Esteve, Sofia Fonseca and, in particular, Gemma Bové who carried out the English translation.

Finally, I would like to thank Dr. John Taylor from the British Museum and Dr. Geofrey T. Martin from the University of Cambridge for kindly supporting this publication, and David Davison for his editorial advice and assistance in preparing this monograph.

Montmeló, July 2008

ACKNOWLEDGEMENTS

I would like to take the opportunity to acknowledge all the people who supported me throughout the years of working on this doctoral thesis.

I am grateful to my supervisor, Dr. Rosa Lamuela, for supporting me during the research process; to Dr. Ana Romero for her critical comments and constant advise, and Dr. Maite Ibern for being close to me while sampling, carrying out analytical work and writing; to Dr. Olga Jáuregui from the Scientific and Technical Services of the University of Barcelona, for introducing me to mass spectrometry; to my friends and colleagues of the Nutrition and Food Science Department: Neus, Tresa, Valentina, Delphine, Eva and Mireia.

I wish to thank Dr. Josep Cervelló, my first professor of Egyptology, for encouraging me to go on with Egyptology; to all my Egyptology lecturers: Alberto Quevedo, Montse Díaz de Cerio, Francesca Berenguer, Dr. Rosa Valdesogo, Dr. Marcelo Campagno and Dr. Josep Montserrat.

I would like also to mention the financiers of this project, Mr. Jordi Raventós and Mrs. Virginie Tibau from Codorníu, and Mr. Emilio Castro and the Founders of the Spanish Foundation for Wine Culture, for their interest and kind support.

I would like to express my gratitude to the Egyptian Museum in Cairo (Egypt) for allowing me to consult their archives and for authorising the sampling; to the people working there who assisted me: last General-Director Dr. Mamdouh El-Damaty, curators Mrs. Halla Hassan, Mr. Sayed Hassan, Mr. Adel Mahmoud, Mr. Mahmoud Halwagy, Dr. Nadja Lokma, Mr. Waheed Eduard and Mr. Mahmoud Ibrahim; to the people from the Museum comittees and the policemen of the Egyptian Supreme Council for Antiquities who worked with us during sampling of the amphorae.

Thanks are due to the Egyptian Supreme Council for Antiquities' personnel who helped me to deal with authorities and, specially, to the last secretary-General Dr. G.A. Gaballa.

I would like to acknowledge the Department of Ancient Egypt and Sudan of the British Museum in London (UK), the director Mr. W.V. Davies, his secretary Mrs. Allison Cameron and, in particular, Dr. John Taylor for granting me the authorisation to take samples and allowing me access to the library.

I also wish to thank the authorities of the libraries who allowed me to use their archives: the Special and Rare Collections library in the American University in Cairo; The Egypt Exploration Society in London; the Institut Français d'Archéologie Orientale in Cairo; Montserrat's Monestry library in Catalonia; the Bodleian library in Oxford's University; the Egyptological library of the University of Barcelona; and the Biblioteca de Catalunya in Barcelona.

Special mention to my friends Gemma Bové and Núria Llonch who hosted me in London and Oxford respectively, during my stay in Britain; to my friends-colleagues of Pharmacy faculty: Maite, Sílvia, Laura Guitart and Núria Jiménez.

To Liam Taylor for your good comments and patience in assisting me with English language while preparing three of my articles.

To Waheed for great help despite the distance between Cairo and Barcelona, and to Huda for revising and checking bibliography in Basel.

I wish to thank friends and colleagues from my Egyptology studies: Mikel, David, Meritxell, Beatriz, Luïsa, Cristina; also Sofia, Montse Esteve and Gemma, as well as Montse Godia. For the nice time we had toguether and funny adventurous trips in Egypt.

Finally, to my dear mother because anything I can write here is not enough to say how thankful I am for your constant support, and to my dear father, whom I know is always so close to me.

To the Egyptian land, the *Ta-meri*
(the "Beloved land")

TABLE OF CONTENTS

LIST OF FIGURES

The figures listed here are numbered according to the chapter they belong to.

Figure 4.10. Harvest and winemaking scene. Upper part: grape harvest and foot press. Middle part: sack press and men filling wine jars while a scribe registers it. Lower part: traps to hunt birds. Tomb of Khety [num. 17] in Beni Hassan, 11th Dynasty, Middle Kingdom (Newberry, 1894). Courtesy of the Egypt Exploration Society.

Figure 4.11. Harvest final scene depicting a sack press and traps to catch birds; the rest is damaged. To the left, we observe a heating and filtration process of a liquid through a fabric, that could be a unique representation of the elaboration of *Shedeh*. Tomb of Baqet [num. 15] in Beni Hassan, 11th Dynasty, Middle Kingdom (Newberry, 1894). Courtesy of the Egypt Exploration Society.

Figure 4.12. Harvest and winemaking scene. Upper part: grapes are gathered, pressed in a vat and further pressed in a sack press. Beside, grape baskets are being counted and a scribe records the total amount. Lower part: amphorae are filled up and sealed while a supervisor controls it. On the right-hand side, goats are grazing the vineyard. Tomb of Amenemhat [num. 2] in Beni Hassan, 12th Dynasty, Middle Kingdom (Newberry, 1893). Courtesy of the Egypt Exploration Society.

Figure 4.13. Grape harvest. A standing man supervises the job of labourers and tastes the grapes. Tomb of Intef [TT 155] in Dra Abu el-Naga, Western Thebes, 18th Dynasty, New Kingdom (Säve-Söderbergh, 1957). Copyright: Griffith Institute, University of Oxford.

Figure 4.14. Workers empty the baskets filled with grapes into the press where a group of men tied to ropes, tread the grapes while dancing. Tomb of Intef [TT 155] in Dra Abu el-Naga, Western Thebes, 18th Dynasty, New Kingdom (Säve-Söderbergh, 1957). Copyright: Griffith Institute, University of Oxford.

Figure 4.15. Goddess Hathor, Lady of Thebes, carries an offering with grapes, among others. Nakht's Tomb [TT 52] in Sheikh Abd el-Qurna, Western Thebes, 18th Dynasty, New Kingdom.

Figure 4.16. On the right-hand side, some amphorae are filled with fermenting must while others are already sealed. On the left-hand side, goddess Renenutet dominates the winemaking scene. Tomb of Intef [TT 155] in Dra Abu el-Naga, Western Thebes, 18th Dynasty, New Kingdom (Säve-Söderbergh, 1957). Copyright: Griffith Institute, University of Oxford.

Figure 4.17. A sack press with the two attached poles. Tomb of Intef [TT 155] in Dra Abu el-Naga, Western Thebes, 18th Dynasty, New Kingdom (Säve-Söderbergh, 1957). Copyright: Griffith Institute, University of Oxford.

Figure 4.18. A woman offers wine to a seated male figure who tastes it. The right scene represents the transport of amphorae to the cellar by porters who hold them by their handles. Tomb of Intef [TT 155] in Dra Abu el-Naga, Western Thebes, 18th Dynasty, New Kingdom (Säve-Söderbergh, 1957). Copyright: Griffith Institute, University of Oxford.

Figure 4.19. Wine vessels had two handles to be held during their transport; amphorae were then stored in a cellar. Tomb of Intef [TT 155] in Dra Abu el-Naga, Western Thebes, 18th Dynasty, New Kingdom (Säve-Söderbergh, 1957). Copyright: Griffith Institute, University of Oxford.

Figure 4.20. A man seals an amphorae by placing a pottery lid on its mouth. Tomb of Khaemuaset (TT 261) in Western Thebes, 18th Dynasty, New Kingdom (Hope, 1993). Copyright: Griffith Institute, University of Oxford.

Figure 4.21. Drawing of a clay seal of a New Kingdom amphora. It is a cylindrical seal made of clay that covers the mouth and neck of the amphora entirely. Under it, one can also observe the rush stopper on top of the mouth (Hope, 1993). Copyright: Griffith Institute, University of Oxford.

Figure 4.22. The clay seal was stamped with the name of the product and the estate where it was coming from. Tomb of Parennefer (TT 188) in Western Thebes, 18th Dynasty, New Kingdom (Hope, 1993). Copyright: Griffith Institute, University of Oxford.

Figure 4.23. Inscription in amphora JE 62313 from Tutankhamon's collection, in the Egyptian Museum in Cairo. The upper part, written in hieratic script, reads: "Year 5. Wine from the Estate of Tutankhamun, Ruler of Southern On, l.p.h., [in] the Western River. Chief vintner Khaa." The lower part, indicates the same inscription in hieroglyph writing (Černy, 1965). Copyright: Griffith Institute, University of Oxford.

Figure 4.24. Storeroom of the royal palace full of amphorae; men are waving fans to refresh the environment. Tomb of Parennefer at el-Amarna, Akhenaten's reign, 18th Dynasty, New Kingdom (Davies, 1908). Courtesy of the Egypt Exploration Society.

Figure 5.1. Wine jar Cairo Museum number JE 62303 found at the Annexe chamber of Tutankhamun's tomb [KV 62] at Western Thebes. The inscription reads: "Year 4. Wine from the Estate of Aten, l.p.h., in the Western River. Chief vintner Nen". The clay seal is broken and it is open on its upper part. Copyright: Maria Rosa Guasch Jané, with permission from the Egyptian Museum in Cairo.

Figure 5.2. Tutankhamun's amphorae displayed at the Egyptian Museum in Cairo. Copyright: Maria Rosa Guasch Jané, with permission from the Egytian Museum in Cairo.

Figure 5.3. Pentu had several titles during Akhenaten's reign [1.353-1.336 BC]: royal scribe, chief of the servers of Aten in Aten's Temple in Akhetaten, chief of doctors and private counsellor, among others. Lintel of the tomb of Pentu [num. 5] in el-Amarna, 18th Dynasty, New Kingdom (Davies, 1906). Courtesy of the Egypt Exploration Society.

Figure 6.1. Papyrus Salt 825 [BM 10051], in the British Museum in London, describing the preparation of the *Shedeh*: "This is [...] repeat the filtration, heating again. This is the way how *Shedeh*, which Ra has given to his sons, is made". Due to a damage in the papyrus on the right side below, the starting product –the raw material- is unknown. The rest of the sentence can be read on the top, left side, from right to left.

Figure 6.2. Inscription on amphora Cairo Museum JE 62315: "Year 5. Very good quality *Shedeh* from the Estate of Aten in the Western River. Chief vintner Rer" being the quality "very good" emphasised on its upper part. This amphora was found by Howard Carter in between the shrine and the south wall of the Burial chamber of Tutankhamun's tomb [KV 62] at Western Thebes, and it belongs now to the collection of the Egyptian Museum in Cairo. Copyright: Griffith Institute, University of Oxford.

LIST OF TABLES AND FIGURES EXPERIMENTAL PART

Table 1. Archaeological samples collected from ancient Egyptian pottery jars.

Table 2. LC/MS/MS optimum condition for tartaric acid and syringic acid MS/MS detection in the negative mode.

Figure A. Production of syringic acid. Syringic acid is released from the flavilium structure of malvidin-3-glucoside in the polymerized pigment by alkaline fusion through the formation of a hydrated hemichemical form in which the pyran (C ring) is broken in two steps.

Figure B. Total ion chromatogram [TIC] in full-scan mode for tartaric acid in CM1 sample scanning from 100 to 250 u.

Figure C. LC/MS/MS chromatogram in SIM mode for tartaric acid in CM1 sample.

Figure D. LC/MS/MS chromatogram in MRM mode using m/z 149→87 transition for tartaric acid in CM1 sample.

Figure E. LC/MS/MS chromatogram in MRM mode using m/z 149→87 transition for tartaric acid (TA) peak in BM1 and BM2 samples.

Figure F. LC/MS/MS chromatogram in MRM mode using m/z 149→87 transition for tartaric acid (TA) peak in CM2 sample and the blank. No tartaric acid is present in the blank.

Figure G. LC/MS/MS chromatogram in MRM mode using m/z 149→87 transition for tartaric acid in BM3 sample.

Figure H. LC/MS/MS chromatogram in MRM mode using m/z 149→87 transition for tartaric acid (TA) in BM3 sample spiked with standard of tartaric acid.

Figure I. LC/MS/MS chromatogram in MRM mode using m/z 197→182 transition for syringic acid in CM1 sample before and after the alkaline oxidation, and for the standard of syringic acid. Syringic acid is present after the alkaline reaction of the CM1 sample.

Figure J. LC/MS/MS chromatogram in MRM mode using m/z 149→87 transition for tartaric acid is identified in the sample from the *Shedeh* amphora.

Figure K. LC/MS/MS chromatogram in MRM mode using m/z 197→182 transition for syringic acid, before and after the alkaline reaction, in the sample from the *Shedeh* amphora. The red grape marker syringic acid is not present in the sample before the alkaline oxidation, as it is in a more complex form. By performing the alkaline reaction to the sample, a peak of syringic acid is identified having been released from malvidin-3-glucoside in the pigment.

Figure L. LC/MS/MS chromatograms in MRM mode for the EM5 sample of residue from the amphora JE 62314 found beside the west wall at the Burial chamber of Tutankhamun's tomb [KV 62] in Western Thebes. (a) The grape marker tartaric acid is identified in the sample. (b) After performing alkaline fusion to the sample, the red grape marker syringic acid, derived from malvidin-3-glucoside, is also identified.

Figure M. LC/MS/MS chromatograms in MRM mode for the EM2 sample from the amphora JE 62302 inscribed "Visir Pentu". (a) The grape marker tartaric acid is identified in the sample. (b) After performing alkaline fusion to the sample, syringic acid derived from malvidin is not detected.

Figure N. LC/MS/MS chromatograms in MRM mode for the EM4 sample from the amphora JE 62312 inscribed "Sweet wine". (a) The grape marker tartaric acid is identified in the sample. (b) After performing alkaline fusion to the sample, syringic acid derived from malvidina-3-glucoside is not detected in the sample.

I. INTEREST AND OBJECTIVES

Wine is a beverage that belongs to the Mediterranean culture. A study of the origins of wine shows how deep vineyards are rooted in this area from West to East and since antiquity.

The oldest and most extensive documentation about viticulture and winemaking comes from Egypt. Vineyards have been grown in the Nile Delta for five thousand years. The historical and archaeological study of documents and paintings related to winemaking coming from walls of Egyptian tombs, still presents nowadays unknown aspects. Thanks to the development of analytical techniques, we are now able to shed light on a new aspect known to us from the first Mediterranean civilization: the wine culture in Egypt.

Ancient Egyptians lived in a priviledged environment: the Delta and the Valley of the Nile. Part of their history has arrived to us thanks to their particular conception of death and the Afterlife.

Wine in ancient Egypt was a prestigious product consumed only by the upper classes and the royal family. Wine jars were placed in tombs as offerings to the dead in order for them to be able to enjoy this drink in the Afterlife. Thanks to the existence of decorated scenes on walls of Egyptian tombs showing the elaboration of wine, we are able to know how it was made.

During the New Kingdom period [1.539-1.075 BC] (dates according to Baines and Malek, 2002), wine jars were identified in a similar way to wine bottles at present: with the help of labels. The data written on them was giving information about the product: the vintage as a year of reign, the area of production and its estate, the quality, and the name of the winemaker who was responsible for the elaboration of the wine. The name given to the product was usually wine [*Irp*] but the kind of wine, whether it was red or white, was never noted down on the inscriptions. Nevertheless, another kind of beverage [*Shedeh*] has been found for which no translation exists, being its raw material also unknown. This study starts from these omissions.

The objectives of the present doctoral thesis are:

1. To do a bibliographical study of viticulture and oenology in ancient Egypt.

2. To verify, in an analytical way, the presence of wine in amphorae of ancient Egypt.

    ⤳ To make analysis of tartaric acid -a characteristic wine compound- contained in samples from Egyptian amphorae.

    ⤳ In order to pursue this objective, amphorae dating from three to five thousand years ago and belonging to the collections of the Egyptian Museum in Cairo (Egypt) and the Department of Ancient Egypt and Sudan of the British Museum in London (United Kingdom) will be studied.

3. To investigate what kind of wine was made in ancient Egypt, either red or white.

    To do this it is necessary:

    ⤳ To develop a new method for determining wine markers in archaeological samples. The liquid chromatography coupled to mass spectrometry in tandem technique, which allows high specificity and high sensibility for the compounds, will be used. The new method should allow the identification of tartaric acid, characteristic of grapes and already a wine marker in archaeology, and syringic acid derived from malvidina, as a red wine marker.

    ⤳ To make analysis of dry residues found inside Egyptian amphorae.

4. To identify the raw material of the product kept in amphorae and called *Shedeh* by ancient Egyptians.

    ⤳ To make an analysis of a dry residue found inside an amphora inscribed with the name *Shedeh,* to find out whether this drink was made from grapes or from something else.

II. EGYPTIAN WINE IN CONTEXT

II.1. INTRODUCTION

In the ancient Egyptian civilization, the pharaoh was considered a God living on earth. For him the most impregnable tomb was build and the most valued offerings were made to allow him to follow the path to the Afterlife. Life on earth in good working order depended on it.

Few royal tombs have been found with intact funerary objects as most of them had been plundered already in antiquity. The tomb of King Tutankhamun -despite two robberies occurred some time after its closure- had been exceptionally preserved for more than three thousand three hundred years in the Kings' Valley at Western Thebes (present Luxor) until its famous discovery in 1922 by the English archaeologist Howard Carter.

The young Tutankhamun [1.332-1.322 BC], who reigned in Egypt at the end of the 18th Dynasty, New Kingdom period [1.539-1.075 BC], was buried together with selected products, the most valued products at that time. Among the food and beverage uncovered, there was a collection of wine amphorae.

During the New Kingdom [1.539-1.075 BC], the person in charge of winemaking wrote on the amphorae detailed information about the product they contained. Inscriptions were handwriten in ink in hieratic form (a kind of cursive writing).

Already from the Old Kingdom [2.575-2.150 BC] onwards, tombs of the nobility were decorated with daily scenes, among which we find viticulture and winemaking. These scenes show us the way in which grape harvest and vinification were carried out in Egypt. The amphorae, or containers where wine was kept, were also represented.

Taking these tomb scenes and inscriptions on New Kingdom amphorae as a starting point, it can be deduced that different kinds of wine may have coexisted in ancient Egypt.

But what kind of wines were they?

Neither the inscriptions on amphorae nor ancient Egyptian texts mention the colour of wine. Either ancient Egyptians did not give importance to the colour of wine, or they only manufactured one kind of wine. Considering that wine was associated with the blood of Osiris -the god of resurrection- and that grapes in tomb paintings were painted in a dark color, we could think that all wine was red. However, the existence of red wine in ancient Egypt has not been verified until now.

Different analytical methods previously published have allowed the identification of tartaric acid as a wine marker in archaeological samples. Nevertheless, the low sensibility of these methods required the use of large samples and, in general, these techniques were not very effective in identifing tartaric acid. This can be a problem because archaeological samples are normally available in small amounts. Being archaeological samples always unique, and more often than not belonging to museum collections, each one of them becomes very precious. Because of that, the need to develop a new methodology able to work with the smallest amounts of sample possible arose. Besides, we must take into consideration that none of the already-existing methods allowed to carry out a study of the colour of wine because tartaric acid does not give any information about the kind of grapes. Therefore, it was necessary to establish a marker for red wine in archaeology.

Antocyans are pigments that give colour to red wine while not being present in white wine. Antocyans are unstable and they polimerize with time forming more complex structures. In 1996, Singleton formulated a hypothesis that syringic acid could be used as a wine marker. He proved that from the alkaline fusion of a modern red wine malvidin [malvidin-3-glucoside], as the major antocyan responsible for the colour of red wine, was broken and released syringic acid. According to Singleton (1996), when wine ages malvidin forms polymers that allow it to be preserved for a long time. We considered the use of malvidin as a red wine marker in archaeological residues because it is characteristic of red wine and it is not present in white wine.

Due to the lack of an analytical method for archaeological residues coming from vinification that would allow us to carry out our investigation, and having the objective of improving and completing it, we have developed a new method. This method had to be highly selective for archaeological residues of wine, and had to work with small quantities of sample.

Among the samples that are going to be studied, there are eight amphorae from the tomb of Tutankhamun, nowadays at the Egyptian Museum in Cairo (Egypt). Residues were found inside of them. These amphorae are exceptionally well-preserved and they have an incalculable archaeological value.

II.2. LIFE IN ANCIENT EGYPT

Egyptian landscape is extraordinary because although it is geographically within the Sahara desert and close to the tropic of Cancer, the River Nile flows through the country from south to north. In the past, the Nile helped to avoid great problems like the lack of water. The fertility of the Egyptian land did not come from rain, which decreased suddenly at the end of the humid phase of the Neolithic period [about 2.350 BC], but from the annual "miracle" of the River Nile (Stroudhal, 1992). The cicle of life depended on the annual flood of the Nile. The characteristics of the territory where ancient Egyptians lived conditioned their funerary believes. In order to undestand the way in which Egyptians lived, we should consider first where they inhabited.

Ancient Egyptians divided their land into the Black land [khemet], where growing all kind of plants and trees was possible, and the Red land [desheret] or the desert, where no life was possible.

The Nile was part of Egyptians' life and all agriculture activities were performed according to it. Daily life depended on the flooding of the Nile because its contribution of mud fertilised the land allowing the growth of all kinds of crop that fed the population. Not only did the Nile provide with the water that made life possible but it also had a deep influence on the whole country.

The place where the Nile was born was unknown until its discovery in the middle of the 19th century.

As a convention, the source of the River Nile is considered to be the Rippon Waterfalls, which is the natural way out of the Victoria Lake that was formed in the middle of the African fault of the Great Rift, between Uganda, Kenya and Tanzania, in central Africa. But it is further south, in Burundi, where the furthest part of the Nile is, the River Kasumo. The Kasumo, 6.700 Km away from its mouth into the Mediterranian Sea, becomes the River Kagera that, on its turn, flows into the Victoria Lake. Its water comes from the thaw of the Mountains of the Moon [Ruwenzori], situated between Uganda and the Democratic Republic of Congo, and under permanent equatorial fogs (Pavitt, 2001).

The tropical rains provided the River Nile with a volume of water relatively constant during the whole year. The river received different names along its course: from the way out of the Albert Lake until Khartum (capital city of Sudan) it was known as the White Nile and there, it was joined to the Blue Nile, becoming the Nile or Great Nile. The Blue Nile was considered to start at the Tissisat Waterfalls, which are the way out of the Tana Lake in Ethiopia, although the Abbai River was its main tributary.

The Nile has a tributary, the River Atbara, which starts at the mountains in the north of Ethiopia and flows into the Nile in the north of Khartum, in Sudan.

Strictly speaking, the Nile Valley ends to the north of the modern city of Cairo where the river expands forming the Nile Delta until the Mediterranian Sea. In antiquity, the Nile Delta had seven branches but nowadays there are only two, named Rosetta and Damietta. One of the ancient branches was called the "Western River", and it was located in the western side of the Delta next to the modern city of Alexandria.

Both the Blue Nile and the Atbara rivers received a huge flow of water from the summer monsoon of the Ethiopian mountains -being in fact the main supply of water to the River Nile- that further increased the level of the Nile on its way through Egypt and the Delta, from July to October (Baines, 2002).

II.2.1. THE NILE FLOODING

In ancient Egypt, the water level of the Nile reached its lowest point from April to June. The flood started in July and increased quickly in August. The highest point was in the middle of August in Upper Egypt and around middle October in the Delta (Vercoutter, 1992). The flood allowed washing salts out of the soil depositing a stratum of sediments of black color, black earth, that fertilized the land (Baines and Malek, 2002). The deposit, which was a dense and humid mud, was being accumulated year after year at a rate of several centimeters per century (Baines and Malek, 2002).

During the flood, work in the fields stopped and people took advantage of it by fishing, bird hunting and visiting their family and friends; that was the moment when grapes were ready to be picked up (Wilkinson, 1998).

By astronomical observation, Egyptians knew that the star Sirius, also called Sothis [Spdt], reappeared on the eastern horizon around the 18th of July together with the sun, after forty days of having disappeared on the sky; it is the so-called heliac rise of Sirius (Desroches-Noblecourt, 1995). This fact coincided with the start of the flood, so that the reappearance of the star Sirius announced the imminent flooding as well as the beginning of the year (Meeks and Favard-Meeks, 1996). The star Sirius was related to the goddess Isis and played a fundamental role in the life of humanity (Meeks and Favard-Meeks, 1996). According to Egyptian religious beliefs, the flood of the Nile would bring a period of fertility and renovation, simbol of the eternity of Osiris, the god of the dead and resurrection. Feasts and offerings to gods were organised for the occasion. For example, Ramses II is represented offering wine to the divine triad to celebrate the New Year and the Nile flood at the small Temple of Abu

3

Figure 2.1. Pharaoh Tutmosis III making a wine offering to god Sokaris. Deir el-Bahari temple in Western Thebes, 18th Dynasty, New Kingdom. Copyright: Maria Rosa Guasch Jané.

Simbel (Desroches-Noblecourt and Kuenz, 1968). There is also a representation of king Tutmosis III offering wine to god Sokaris in the Temple of Deir el-Bahari, at Western Thebes [Figure 2.1].

The Nile flood was mesured thanks to nilometres or deep pools connected to the Nile that had a graduated wall. Nilometres, built all over Egypt, allowed to know whether the level of the river was satisfactory for the needs of the population as well as being used to calculate the income tax on agriculture. In October or November the water level fell and the River Nile recovered its normal level, leaving a deposit behind that made sowing possible (Baines, 2002).

II.2.2. THE AGRICULTURE AND THE FOOD

Ancient Egyptians had an agricultural calendar appart from the solar and lunar ones. This agricultural calendar had three seasons: the season of the flood [*akhet*]; the winter season [*peret*], this was the sowing time because the ground reappeared after flooding; and the harvest season [*shemu*] or summer (Vercoutter, 1992).

Every year people hoped for a satisfactory level of flood, not too high to inundate the areas where people lived in, and not too low because then it would not provide enough lime and it would cause a lack of water (Wilkinson, 1998). A drainage system existed to increase the extension of cultivable land distributing water to areas where, in general, the flood did not reach. They could be low lands that were only inundated during years of

exceptionally high flood or far away grounds that would never be flooded. Crops were different in each one of them: vegetables were seasonal and it was necessary to water them in abundance; that is why they were grown next to the water in fertilised grounds; vineyards, on the contrary, were grown mostly in the high lands.

Nile water could reach higher parts of the territory thanks to the *shaduf*, which consisted on a horizontal stick resting on a pivot that had a counterweight. A container for keeping the water hanged on the other side. We can see it represented in the tombs of Neferhotep and Merira II at el-Amarna, which date from the 18th Dynasty [1.539-1.292 BC], New Kingdom period.

In earlier times, men transported water by carrying a wooden yoke on their shoulders with two jars filled with water hanging from it, as we can see in scenes from the tomb of Mereruka in Saqqara of the 6th Dynasty [2.325-2.175 BC], Old Kingdom period.

A great part of cultivable land was destined to grow cereals to feed people and linen to dress them. There were also fruit and palm trees to provide shadow, as well as vegetables planted in such a way that they divided the land into small squares surrounded by an earthen wall. Once the level of the river was low, the land was irrigated artificially. Water was transported to pools with the help of dykes that could store water by blocking the entrance. In the city of el-Amarna, inhabited at the end of the 18th Dynasty, big public wells were built as well as smaller and

Figure 2.2. A pergola vine supported by wooden columns in the shape of papyruses, and surrounding a pool. Tomb of Khenamun [TT 93] in Western Thebes, 18th Dynasty, New Kingdom (Wilkinson, 1998). Courtesy of the Egypt Exploration Society.

private ones to supply population and animals with water and to allow watering trees and plants from gardens (Kemp, 1992).

Big houses normally had a grapevine planted around a pool [Figure 2.2]. Behind it, there were date palms, sicomor trees and fig trees to offer shade to the house. In the gardens fruit and vegetables were grown to feed the family, the workers and to pay taxes to the temple and the pharaoh. The gardens of the temples provided food for priests and offerings for the cult. The gardens of the palace, as well as the gardens of noble houses, were also ornamental.

As regards food "it is difficult to reconstruct everyday food because we only have archaeological documentation, written as well as figurative, of funerary rituals and banquets organised for special festivities and we can not know what the daily meal of a worker was" (Sist, 1987).

As described by Diodorus in the Greco-Roman period [332BC-395], people who lived in the Delta were particularly well provided thanks to the fruit and vegetables grown there that allowed to cover the necessities of poor and sick people (Garnsey, 1999). For Garnsey (1999) the Nile is the main singularity of Egypt and the source of its varied, rich and plentiful diet.

Cereals were the base of the quotidian diet, from which bread and beer were made. There was a great variety of vegetables and fruit that were cultivated in the orchards: onion, garlic, lettuce, cucumber, melon, and also pulses such as beans and lentils. From palm and fruit trees all sort of

fruits were obtained: dates from palm trees could be eaten either fresh or dried, sicomor figs, walnuts of the *doum* palm and pomegranates as well. The vine provided grapes that were considered delicious to eat either fresh or sundried –raisins- although winemaking was its common use.

The main source of proteins for most of the people came from fishing and hunting wild birds: ducks, geese, storks, finches, cranes and pigeons (Wilson, 2001). Some birds were raised in aviaries with the purpose of obtaining eggs (Wilson, 2001). Goat and lamb was only consumed on special occasions (Stroudhal, 1992). For upper class people, diet could include ox, antelope and gazelle (Stroudhal, 1992). The consumption of pork was already avoided before 3.200 BC [Predynastic period] in Upper Egypt while that was not the case in Lower Egypt (Menguin and Amer, 1932). With the unification of Egypt the tradition of avoiding pork spread to the Nile Valley and the Delta ("The Cambridge", 2000). According to Stroudhal (1992) meat could be boiled, roasted or fried in either oil or a kind of butter while fish was normally grilled.

Goats and sheep supplied with milk for children and young people mostly, but it was also used to prepare a kind of yogurt and cheese (Wilson, 2001). Honey was highly appreciated as a sweetener. Oil, garlic and salt were used for cooking. Salt was also used in order to preserve meat and fish. Another way to preserve food was sun-drying it, mainly fruit and fish. They also used spices like cinnamon, anise, rosemary and coriander (Stroudhal, 1992).

Figure 2.3. Family scene where king Akhenaten and queen Nefertiti with princesses Ankhesenpaaten (who would later on marry Tutankhamun) and Meritaten, are seating opposite their guests: queen mother Tiyi and her daughter Baketaten. The king, Nefertiti and the queen mother drink wine served in wine glasses. Tomb of Huya in el-Amarna, 18th Dynasty, New Kingdom (Davies, 1905). Courtesy of the Egypt Exploration Society.

Lower class people used to eat twice a day, in the morning and in the evening and they did it on low tables. There was a common plate from which everybody ate either with their hands or with the aid of bread. Both before and after eating they would wash their hands with water and, mostly in the case of upper class people, they would also rinse their mouth with salty water after their meal (Stroudhal, 1992).

Wealthy people used to seat on chairs at a small table where an individual service was set but with no cutlery (Stroudhal, 1992). Servants would bring water to wash their hands first, and then would serve food and fill the wine glasses. This procedure can be seen in many banquet scenes represented on walls of New Kingdom tombs in Western Thebes, where one can also notice that meals were accompanied by dance and music. In some Amarna tombs the royal family is represented during their meals; they are daily scenes of pharaoh Akhenaten and his family, fact that had never been shown in earlier periods. In the tomb of Huya at el-Amarna, the royal family is shown drinking wine at dinner [Figure 2.3].

II.2.3. FUNERARY BELIEFS AND BURIALS

Ancient Egyptians attached great importance to food both during their wordly life and their afterlife.

Death was considered to be the step from earthly life to another life. Religious beliefs of ancient Egyptians required the body of the deceased to be preserved during burials. For this reason, the body was embalmed and surrounded by every day objects taken from this life but necessary in the Afterlife as well; besides the body would also need to eat.

The death and burial of Egyptian kings was an event of cosmic significance (Taylor, 2001).

Ancient Egyptians believed that the cosmos would not be in order until the dead king would be buried with proper rites that would allow him to enjoy afterlife among the gods (Taylor, 2001).

Therefore, a tomb that would lodge the body of the dead king was built and funerary offerings placed inside in such a way that he would be able to enjoy them for eternity.

In Upper Egypt during the Predynastic period, the figure of the king was identified with the god Horus, in life, and the god Osiris in death (Cervelló, 1996). The king would assure the maintainance of cosmic order [*maat*]. He would be a participant of the collective osiriac destinies beyond the grave and his subjects would simply share the same destiny; they would be saved and would resurrect thanks to him, to go to a world beyond the grave in which he would still be their king and they would still be his subjects for all eternity (Cervelló, 1996).

Royal burials in Predynastic Upper Egypt [in Nekhen, Qustul, Nagada and Abydos] were built in the shape of a house, called "mastaba", and made of adobe [a mixture of earth and straw dried in the sun]. By contrast, it seems that in Predynastic Lower Egypt there was a sun cult in the city of On [Heliopolis] if we consider the position of the bodies found in the necropolis facing East (Vandier, 1952).

In unified Egypt, during the 1st and 2nd Dynasties [2.950-2.650 BC], the royal tombs of Abydos and Saqqara were mastabas following the osiriac cult. During the 3rd Dynasty [2.650-2.575 BC] the solar theology of Heliopolis was adopted by the royalty so that the king obtained new afterlife destinies both celestial and solar, exclusively for him, while those of the people would continue to be osiriac (Cervelló, 1996). On the one hand, the new sun doctrine kept the political aspect of Osiris that identified him with the figure of the king-father-dead; its fertility aspect that connected him to vegetation, fertilising waters and flood; and its astral aspect that indentified him with Orion (Cervelló, 1996). But on the other hand, the earthly and funerary aspects of Osiris were rejected because they were going against the heliopolitan ideas of how a royal tomb should be (Cervelló, 1996). The new funerary monument of the Old Kingdom [2.575-2.150 BC] built for the king was the pyramid, from the end of the 3rd Dynasty onwards and mainly during the 6th Dynasty [2.325-2.175 BC]. It was the result of this combination between upper Egyptian tradition and solar theology of Heliopolis: a pyramid structure of solar tradition with an underground substructure like the case of the three pyramids at Giza from the 4th Dynasty [2.575-2.450 BC].

Inside of Unas pyramid at Saqqara, from the 5th Dynasty [2.450-2.325 BC], Egyptian afterlife beliefs were for the first time recorded in the Pyramid Texts. During the 6th Dynasty, smaller pyramids with big funerary temples were built where priests would perform the daily cult of the pharaoh.

From the Middle Kingdom period [1.975-1.640 BC] onwards, high rank officials and nobility were buried in rock tombs.

In the New Kingdom [1.549-1.075 BC] kings and nobility were buried in rock tombs on the west bank of the river, inside the hills of Thebes [nowadays Luxor]. They had no superstructure even though the explanation might be that the hilltop of el-Qurn acted as a superstructure for all tombs (Taylor, 2001).

The royal tomb during the New Kingdom period consisted of a funeray chamber housing the stone sarcophagus of the dead king and several storerooms. Its walls were decorated with scenes describing the stages of the trip that the king would have to go through on his way to the underground world. During this trip, the sun, and the dead king by assimilation, was travelling by night and reappeared rejuvenated the next morning (Taylor, 2001). The death of the pharaoh meant the victory of chaos over order [*maat*]. For this reason, when a king died a new successor had to be appointed and proclaimed king as soon as possible, at sunrise the day after the death of the previous pharaoh (Taylor, 2001).

Upper class members, in contrast with royalty, decorated their tombs with daily life scenes already since the Old Kingdom. Some of these representations were the manufacture and transport of objects and offerings to the tomb, or the noble himself hunting wild birds, fishing or supervising field works in his property. These land activities could be the growing of cereals, fruit trees or vineyards. Officials' tombs had a "false door" that connected this world with the afterlife. In front of it, family members offered food on an offering table and the *ka* of the deceased received them.

II.3. TUTANKHAMUN

Tutankhamun was born in Akhetaten [modern el-Amarna, in Middle Egypt] under the name of *Tut-Ankh-Aten* [Living Image of Aten] during the second half of Akhenaten's reign [1.353-1.336 BC] at the end of the 18th Dynasty.

The lineage of Tutankhamun has been discussed by many authors. There has been a lot of speculation about whether he had royal origin, whether he was a son or a half brother of pharaoh Akhenaten, or even if he was related at all to the royal family. An inscription on a stone block coming from the Great Temple of Aten in el-Amarna, but found at Hermopolis, says: "son of the king, of his body, *Tut-Ankhu-Aten*", confirming its royal origin (Vandersleyen, 1995). According to this, Tutankhamun would be a son of king Akhenaten, but who his mother was or could be is left out.

Akhenaten and Queen Nefertiti were often represented together with their daughters in tombs and temples at el-Amarna. This could make us suppose that Nefertiti had not had any son yet. Akhenaten's second wife, Kiya, had the title "Much Beloved Wife" and could have been Tutankhaten's mother. In fact, by the time Tutankhaten was born she disappeared from the records and it is thought that she might have died while giving birth (Reeves, 1990). But later on, this supposition became doubtful and Gabolde (1993) suggested the possibility that, in fact and against what had been earlier supposed, Tutankhaten was the son of Queen Nefertiti.

Pharaoh Akhenaten was succeeded by Ankheperure Nefernefruaten [1.336-1.335 BC], who could have been Queen Nefertiti acting as a regent because, actually, her second name was Nefernefruaten (Reeves, 1992). But this could also have been her oldest daughter, Merytaten (Gabolde, 1998). Once Akhenaten died, it was necessary to name a successor who would marry the queen. The existence of a letter sent by the queen of Egypt (Merytaten or maybe Nefertiti) to the king of the Hittites asking him to send one of his sons to marry her has been documented. He was probably killed before arriving in Egypt. According to Gabolde (1998), this person who married the Queen of Egypt would have been Smenkhare, to whom an ephemeral reign, from 1.335-1.332 BC, is attributed.

Although documentation from the Amarna period is more extensive than the one from the other ancient Egyptian periods, it is more fragmented (Gabolde, 1998).

After a short reign of these two figures, Ankheperure Nefernefruaten and Smenkhare, whose royal relationship have been the object of discussion until now, Tutankhaten was appointed as the king of Egypt.

Tutankhaten married Ankhesenpaaten, the third daughter of Akhenaten and Nefertiti. When he reached the throne he must have been about eight years old and, according to the inscriptions on wine jars refering to the grape harvest of the ninth year of his reign, he must have reigned in Egypt for at least nine complete years and, accordingly, he would have died during the tenth year (Černy, 1964). Because of his young age, his government was directed by others: on one side there was Ay, holding the title of "God's father", who succeeded Tutankhamun as a Pharaoh [Ay's reign: 1.332-1.319 BC] and, on the other side, General Horemheb, who would later on succeed Ay on the throne [Horemheb's reign: 1.319-1.292 BC] (Eaton-Krauss, 1986).

The most famous event of Tutankhamun's reign [1.332-1.322 BC] is the restoration of goods and properties to the temples after the reign of Akhenaten, and the move of Egypt's administrative capital from el-Amarna to Memphis, while Thebes recovered the status of religious capital. The capital city of el-Amarna was probably abandoned when the king decided to change his own name by substituting God Aten for Amun, the god of Thebes (Vandersleyen, 1995). He did it before the grape harvest of the second year, in accordance with written evidence on wine jars (Eaton-Krauss, 1986). In the second year of Tutankhaten's reign all royal names ending in "aten" were changed into "amun" and the worship of god Amun and the rest of traditional gods was reestablished (Reeves, 1992). Gabolde and Eaton-Krauss (Gabolde, 1998) agree in that the king could have left el-Amarna once he reached the throne due to the lack of documentation bearing his name in palaces, temples and properties at el-Amarna. Vandersleyen (1995) had already pointed it out, giving the reason that the coronation name of Tutankhamun had the epithet "Head of the Southern-Heliopolis" refering to the city of Thebes.

Tutankhamun's death was unexpected as shows the fact that he was quickly buried by Ay (Reeves, 1992) in a tomb that was not the one being built for him at the Western Valley of Thebes [WV 23] but in a smaller one at the Kings' Valley [KV 62]. Later, Ay would use his tomb at the Western Valley to be buried in it. While during the reign of Ay, Tutankhamun's memory was still honoured, during the reign of Horemheb his memory was prosecuted and Tutankhamun's name was changed in statues and other representations; however, the mummy of the king, his funerary equipment and his tomb were saved from it (Eaton-Krauss, 1986).

According to Desroches-Noblecourt (1963), the treasure of Tutankhamun's tomb reveals the level of evolution of the ancient Egyptians, their customs and rites, but not the history of Tutankhamun.

II.3.1. THE DISCOVERY OF THE TOMB

The discovery of the intact tomb of Tutankhamun was due to several circumstances.

Around year 1.140 BC [20th Dynasty, New Kingdom period], workers who were digging the tomb of Ramses VI [KV 9] at the Valley of the Kings threw the remaining material in such a way that it blocked up the entrance of a small tomb that had been forgotten for two centuries (Vercoutter, 1989).

On the other hand, in 1891 the English Howard Carter [1.874-1.939] went to Egypt for the first time contracted by the Archaeological Survey of the Egypt Exploration Fund (later Egypt Exploration Society) in order to help Percy E. Newberry to copy the reliefs and inscriptions from the tombs of Beni Hassan and el-Bersha in Middle Egypt and, later on, at el-Amarna (James, 2001). In 1893, he worked with Edward Naville at the temple of Deir el-Bahari in Western Thebes, where he fell in love with the Valley of the Kings. Soon after he started to work for the Antiquities Survey of Egypt [later Egyptian Supreme Council for Antiquities], he was appointed inspector of the Upper Egypt, advising Theodore Davies, an American millionaire, to excavate the Valley of the Kings in the hope that there could still be found some royal tombs that had been saved from looting. Carter directed and supervised Davies' excavations during which he discovered two plundered tombs: those of Queen Hatshepsut and King Tutmosis IV, from the 18th Dynasty (Vercoutter, 1989). In 1903, he became inspector of Lower and Middle Egypt and he moved to a place near Cairo, but a conflict with a group of tourists who were visiting the Serapeum in Saqqara obliged him to resign from his function. From then on, Carter spent his time painting Egyptian landscapes for tourists. At that time, a well-off English lord, lord Carnarvon, arrived in Egypt to spend the winter far away from cold and humid England and he started to get interested in archaeological excavations to entertain himself. But lord Carnarvon did not have any archaeological knowledge and the director of the Egyptian Antiquities Service, Gaston Maspero, advised him to contract Carter (Vercoutter, 1989). This is how the search for a new tomb started.

In 1907 they excavated in Assuan and afterwards in West Thebes, in the Valley of the Nobles, where they worked until 1914, when Davies' concession to work at the Valley of the Kings expired. Davies did not originally renew it because he though that there was nothing else to be discovered, but Carter seized the opportunity and convinced lord Carnarvon to continue (Vercoutter, 1989). Since 1915 they worked in Amenophis III tomb at the West Valley and, from 1917, at the Valley of the Kings looking for an intact tomb (Reeves, 1990). When they were about to quit the investigations because of lack of findings, on November the 4th 1922, the Egyptian workers discovered a stone staircase leading underground (Vercoutter, 1989). It was made of sixteen steps that led to a door still holding the seals of the guards of the royal necropolis and those of a Pharaoh little known until that moment: the "King of Upper and Lower Egypt" *Nebkheprure*, "Son of Re" *Tutankhamun*, ruler of Southern-Heliopolis.

II.3.2. THE TOMB

Tutankhamun's tomb [KV 62] was cut into living rock in the centre of the Valley of Kings at West Thebes. The entrance was bloked off when Carter discovered it, and marks of the seals of the guardians of the necropolis were imprinted on the door's surface for the tomb's owner to achieve protection from the gods (Reeves, 1990). This tomb had suffered two attempts of robbery, soon after the burial of the king. The door seals discovered by Carter belonged to the team who made the burial and also to the ones who restored it after the robberies.

The first robbery took place in the Antechamber and it seems to have been performed by a man working alone in search of metal objects; the second one was more extensive, although brief as well (Reeves, 1990).

Once we go past the tomb's entrance, a descending passage, or corridor, takes us towards the Antechamber which has a north-south orientation and no wall decoration. The Antechamber was before the funeral chamber, it would have been the "waiting hall" room mentioned in later documents of the Ramessid period (Reeves, 1990). This Antechamber contained the furniture for the funerary household: boxes for jewellery, beds, chairs, thrones and cars among other objects.

On the righthand side of the Antechamber's western wall, a door opens towards another small chamber that is called the Annexe. According to Carter (1933), the Annexe chamber was a storeroom for oils, unguents, wine and food, like other small chambers found in royal tombs of the 18th Dynasty.

Behind the dividing wall, located at the north of the Antechamber, there was the Burial chamber [see Figure 3.1], where four golded shrines made of wood, one inside the other, were found. Inside the shrines there was a stone sarcophagus, which contained two golden coffins, one inside the other. Finally, a coffin made of gold contained the King's mummy. The mummy was wearing a gold mask and was surrounded by jewellery. All these objects were found intact by Carter.

The Burial chamber, unlike the other chambers of the tomb, had an east-west orientation and its walls were decorated. Four niches cut into the walls contained the tomb's «magic bricks». In fact, the Burial chamber and the Treasury chamber contained a great variety of magic objects (Reeves, 1990). Surrounding the sarcophagus [Figure 3.1] there were several objects: next to the east wall there were two lamps, two reed and papyrus boxes and a wine-jar; beside the north wall there was a ritual object and eleven magical

Figure 3.1. In Tutankhamun's Burial chamber three wine-jars were located, nowadays they are displayed at the Egyptian Museum in Cairo. Two of them contained wine [*Irp*], one being placed between the shrine and the east wall [JE 62314] and the other one between the shrine and the west wall [JE 62316]. The third amphora, found between the shrine itself and the south wall, contained *Shedeh* (El-Khouli, 1993). In the picture, the east-west axis runs from the bottom to the top, and the north-south axis from right to left. Copyright: Griffith Institute, University of Oxford.

oars; in the northwest corner there was a double shrine and an Anubis fetish in the form of an animal skin «full of solutions for preserving or washing the body» suspended on a pole; beside the west wall there was another wine-jar; in the southwest corner, an amphora inscribed *Shedeh*, a second Anubis fetish and gilded wooden symbols in the shape of the word «awake» (Reeves, 1990). According to Carter (1927), the three amphorae found in the Burial chamber lacked their stoppers and they had probably been opened during the second robbery.

Finally, the Treasury chamber was at the end of the east wall and had a north-south orientation. This chamber contained objects of purely funerary nature and of an intense religious character (Reeves, 1990). There, there was a canopic shrine containing the king's viscera, two mummified fetuses, as well as boxes, caskets and model boats.

II.4. VITICULTURE AND WINEMAKING IN ANCIENT EGYPT

The first evidence of the presence of grapes in Egypt are seeds found in the Predynastic [4.000-3.050 BC] in the settlements of Tell Ibrahim Awad and Tell el-Farain [Buto] (Murray, 2000), located one in the East and the other one in the West of the Nile Delta.

From Predynastic times, vineyards were grown in Egypt mainly in the Nile Delta, but also in the Western oasis and the Nile valley (Meyer, 1986). Ancient Egyptians knew that the most suitable land to plant vineyards was the one that could not be reached by floods. Vineyards were grown near to the Nile, in a non flooding area (Baum, 1988), where land was mainly gravel, and near to alluvial deposits but free from the mud of the valley. The stony lands at the desert border produced the wines with most reputation (Baum, 1988). One of these lands was the area of Lake Mariut, located at the south-west of the modern city of Alexandria. The most famous wine-producing area during the New Kingdom [1.539-1.075 BC] was the "Western River", in the ancient Canopic branch of the Nile at Western Delta, in the south-west of Alexandria. The "Western River" is documented in hundreds of inscriptions on wine amphorae, like for example on the wine jars of the tomb of King Tutankhamun.

Classic Greek and Roman authors like Atheneus of Naukratis, Strabo and Plinius left written evidence of the good taste of Egyptian wines (Lesko, 1977). Atheneus [170-230 AC] -a Greek coming from Naukratis (Egypt) who lived in Rome- wrote a book which consists of a dialogue among the Socratics during a dinner where they talk about the abundance of vine in the area of Lake Mariut. Atheneus (Athenaeus I, 33 d-f) mentioned the grapes of Mariut as being "very good to eat" and he said that the Nile Valley had plenty of vineyards. He indeed talked about the excellent quality of the wine from Mariut [Mareotic wine] - also named Alexandriotic because of the closeness with the city of Alexandria- besides mentioning the Taeniotic wine and the wine from Antilla also near Alexandria; from the Nile Valley he emphasised the wines from Thebes and Coptos (Athenaeus I, 33 d-f).

The oldest and most extensive documentation about the viticulture process and the manufacture of wines comes from Egypt. Viticulture and wine-making scenes were represented in Egyptian tombs since the Old Kingdom period [2.575-2.150 BC] until the Greco-Roman times [332 BC-395]. According to Lerstrup (1992) these scenes are found in:

- 29 tombs and 1 temple of the Old Kingdom, mainly located at Giza and Saqqara.

- 8 tombs dating from the Middle Kingdom, all of them located in Middle Egypt, apart from two.

- 42 tombs of the New Kingdom, all from the Theban necropolis.

- 3 Theban tombs of the Late period.

- 1 tomb of the Greco-Roman period.

We must take into consideration that all these scenes have neither been found together in one tomb nor during a particular period (Lerstrup, 1992). Often, only the most important parts of the elaboration are represented and some of these scenes have arrived to our times in bad conditions of preservation, or even fragmented. One of the most elaborated scenes of viticulture and oenology comes from the tomb of Intef [TT 155] at Dra Abu el-Naga, in the Theban necropolis.

Grape harvest scenes in the Theban tombs are shown together with scenes of fishing at the marshlands. This might be a reference to the most important vineyards during the New Kingdom that were located at the Nile Delta and produced most of the wine of this period (Säve-Söderberg, 1957).

The following is a description of the elements represented on these scenes. First of all we will deal with viticulture and secondly with the wine making method that, as we will see, is very similar to the traditional European one.

II.4.1. VITICULTURE

Tomb scenes show how vine was grown both in temple and palace gardens and how this one was part of agriculture in general (Wilkinson, 1998). Vineyards are often shown surrounded by a wall and within a context of cultivation of vegetables and fruit trees (Lerstrup, 1992), as we can see in Figure 4.1, where sicomor trees and vegetables are together with vineyards.

In the Old Kingdom [2.575-2.150 BC], grapevine is represented as a climbing plant supported on either a pergola or an arch. The pergola consisted in two supports with either U-shape ends or in the shape of a papyrus column that supported a beam that would act as a roof. A vine growing over a pergola can be seen in Old Kingdom tombs like for example the tomb of Zau at Deir el-Gebrawi [Figure 4.2] and the tomb of Pepiankh at Meir [Figure 4.3] of the 6th Dynasty; the presence of viticulture scenes can also be attested during the Middle Kingdom in tombs like that of Tehutihotep at el-Bersheh [Figure 4.4] of the 12th Dynasty. The climbing vine resting on papyrus-shaped columns can be seen in the Theban tomb of Khenamun [Figure 2.2]. The arch-shaped vine seems to appear later on, during the Middle Kingdom [1.975-1.640 BC]. We find it depicted in Khnumhotep's tomb at Beni Hassan [Figure 4.1] from the 12th Dynasty and, mostly, in 18th Dynasty [1.539-1.292 BC] tombs such as that of Nakht [Figure 4.5] and Khaemuaset (Wilson, 2001) in Western Thebes, or Paheri's tomb [Figure 4.6] in el-Kab.

Figure 4.1. An arch grapevine is represented on the upper left-hand side of the picture, in the middle one can see two sycamore trees and on the right-hand side men watering vegetables. A labourer is picking grapes while another one carries two different kinds of basket; there is an inscription bearing his name on the upper left-hand corner: vintner Netkhernakht. Tomb of Khnumhotep [num. 3] at Beni Hassan, 12th Dynasty, Middle Kingdom (Newberry, 1893). Courtesy of the Egypt Exploration Society.

Figure 4.2. Pergola vine. Tomb of Zau at Deir el-Gebrawi, 6th Dynasty, Old Kingdom (Davies, 1902). Courtesy of the Egypt Exploration Society.

Vines in el-Amarna were supported by terracotta pillars and according to Lerstrup (1992), maybe by wooden poles placed in the crossed-like manner that can still be seen nowadays in small vineyards across Egypt. Grapevine is one of the most recurrent ornaments both on tomb ceilings and on vases (Baum, 1988).

According to Cherpion (1999), the existence of wild and cultivated vines in Egypt is documented by decorative ceilings coming from 18th Dynasty tombs in the Theban necropolis. The decoration of grapes and vine leaves in the tomb of Amenemhat [Figure 4.7] represents a cultivated vine whilst, on the other hand, the vine depicted in the tomb of Sennefer [Figure 4.8] would be a wild one because of its irregularities and its freely-disposed sarments (Cherpion, 1999).

Soon afer picking the grapes, the vine leaves would fall down and the vine tree itself would seem dead because it only kept the sarments. Some months later the vine would sprout again. This cycle was compared by ancient Egyptians to the death and resurrection of god Osiris.

The elements refering to the viticulture represented on the walls of Egyptian tombs are the following:

✵ Taking care of the vine

Vines were watered by pouring water into a hole that had been dug around the trunk; the hole had reinforced sides that prevented the water from flowing away (Lesko, 1977). This can be seen in Ptahhotep's tomb in Saqqara [Figure 4.9] from the 6th Dynasty, Old Kingdom. Nevertheless, we cannot be certain that this was a common practice as this activity is scarcely represented. An Old Kingdom text gives an idea about what kind of work was performed: "The gardener brings loads and his arms and neck ache beneath them. In the morning he waters the vegetables and at the evening the vines" (Wilson, 2001).

Birds posed a threat to ripe grapes that were ready to be gathered. Therefore, in order to avoid birds eating grapes, it was necessary to scare them away and hunt them. That is why traps were set the way we see in the tombs of Khety [Figure 4.10] and Baqet [Figure 4.11] in Beni Hassan.

During the last period, after the harvesting, there were goats grazing vineyards, as the tomb of Amenemhat [Figure 4.12] in Beni Hassan shows. Goats were grazing in order to eat the young sprouts of the vine; next to a scene like this, there is a label saying: "goats in charge of grazing vineyards" (Newberry, 1893).

✵ Grape harvest

Grape harvest started in the summer season. Grapes were generally picked by a group of men,

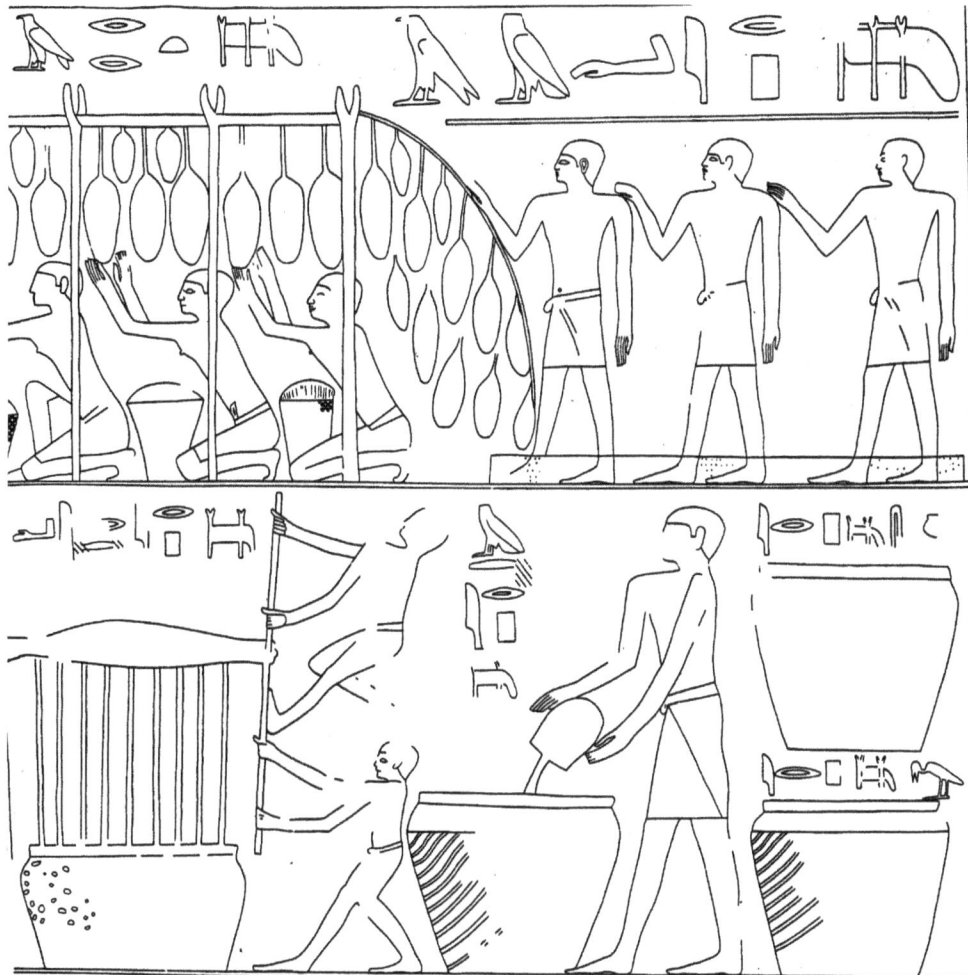

Figure 4.3. Harvest and winemaking scene. The upper part shows a pergola vine on the left-hand side, and three men treading grapes on the right; below, on the left-hand side another group of men is using a sack press. To the right, a man is pouring must in big containers. Tomb of Pepiankh in Meir, 6th Dynasty, Old Kingdom (Blackman and Apted, 1953). Courtesy of the Egypt Exploration Society.

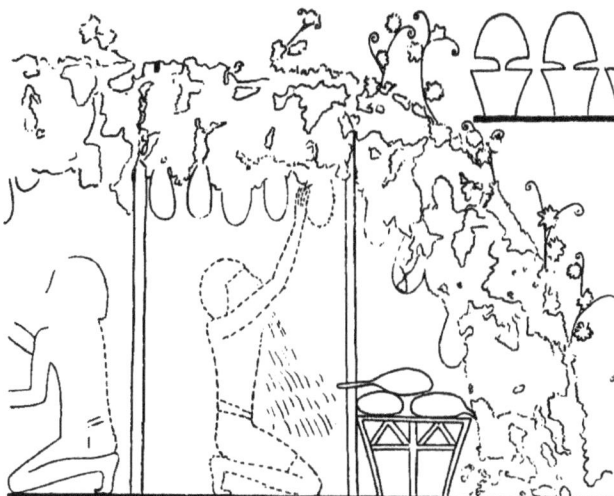

Figure 4.4. Climbing vine and labourers picking up the grapes in a crouching position to store them in baskets. Tomb of Tehutihotep [num. 2] at el-Bersheh, 12th Dynasty, Middle Kingdom (Newberry, s.a.). Courtesy of the Egypt Exploration Society.

although women were also involved, as we can see in the tomb of Paheri [Figure 4.6], and even children, as seen in the tomb of Ptahhotep [Figure 4.9]. We can deduce that vine trees had different heights from the fact that people who were picking grapes are depicted crouching, kneeling or standing. Grapes were picked by hand, without the help of any tool and they were put in baskets, which were placed on the floor beside the worker. According to Meeks (1993) grapes were collected at the end of the day. The reason was probably that temperatures were lower by then being it a key condition to obtain first quality grapes to elaborate wine.

Pepiankh's tomb in Meir [Figure 4.3] from the 6th Dynasty, Tehutihotep's tomb in el-Bersheh [Figure 4.4] from the 12th Dynasty and the Theban tombs of Paheri [Figure 4.6], Intef [Figure 4.13 and 4.14] and Khaemuaset (Wilson, 2001), all three from the 18th Dynasty, depict examples of grape harvest. It is a recurring subject in viticulture and oenology scenes and it seems to be the most significant element for ancient Egyptians, together with the foot press.

Figure 4.5. Grape harvest and winemaking process. Here, an arch-shaped vine has been depicted bearing grapes painted in a dark colour, and men picking them up with their bare hands, without the help of any tool. The dark red must flows out of a pipe into a vat to the right of the foot press. Above, amphorae with two handles can be seen. Nakht's tomb [TT 52] in Sheikh Abd el-Qurna, Western Thebes, 18th Dynasty, New Kingdom.

Figure 4.6. Paheri and his wife receiving offerings. In the upper part there is a harvest and winemaking depiction. Tomb of Paheri at el-Kab, 18th Dynasty, New Kingdom (Tylor and Griffith, 1894). Courtesy of the Egypt Exploration Society.

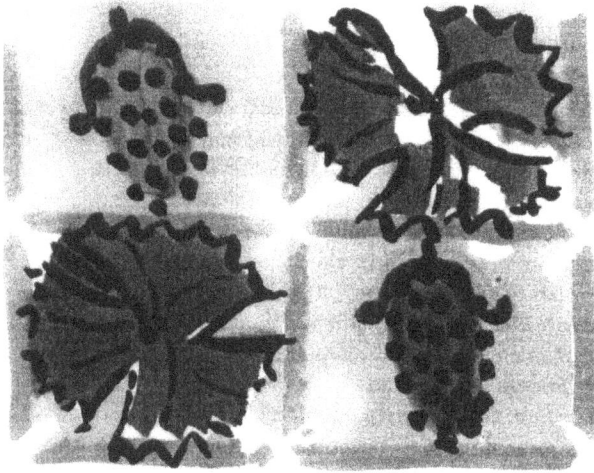

Figure 4.7. Decorative elements representing a cultivated vine. Tomb of Amenemhat [TT 340] at Deir el-Medina, Western Thebes, 18th Dynasty, New Kingdom (Cherpion, 1999). Reproduced wih permission of the Institut Français d'Archéologie Orientale, Cairo.

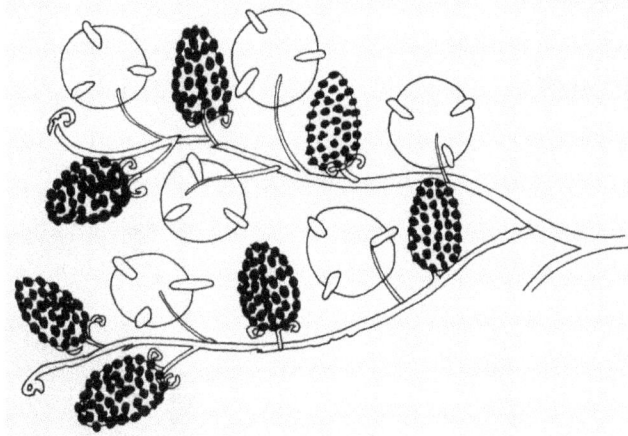

Figure 4.8. Decoration depicting a wild vine. Tomb of Sennefer or "Vines' tomb" [TT 96] in Western Thebes, 18th Dynasty, New Kingdom (Cherpion, 1999). Reproduced wih permission of the Institut Français d'Archéologie Orientale, Cairo.

In the tomb of Intef in Thebes [Figure 4.13], there is an old man supervising the activities of picking and placing grapes in baskets. He appears to be also tasting a grape in order to establish its degree of ripeness, task performed nowadays by enologists. In this unique scene, there was a text next to the figure of the supervisor that would have been a comment made by a labourer, but unfortunately it has not been preserved (Säve-Söderberg, 1957).

Part of the grapes was destined for fresh consume and offerings to the dead, as shown in the Theban tomb of Nakht [Figure 4.15] where goddess Hathor is making an offering with a bunch of grapes. The rest was used for wine making.

❈ **Transport of grapes to the press**

In order to keep the harvested grapes big baskets -probably made of palm leaves- were used, in the same way as wicker baskets were used in Europe to transport grapes until the last century. Baskets could be round like those seen in the tomb of Paheri [Figure 4.6], but also rectangular in the shape of a box as seen in the tomb of Khnumhotep [Figure 4.1].

A scene from Paheri's tomb [Figure 4.6] attests that grapes were immediately put in baskets and carried to the press after being picked. In this way, if any grape burst, its juice would disappear and it would not ferment in contact with the other grapes.

Carriers transported these baskets either on their shoulders, as it is represented in the tomb of Intef [Figures 4.13 and 4.14] or using their arm's strength, according to Paheri's tomb [Figure 4.6]. The above-mentioned scene of Intef gives the impression that the baskets filled with bunches were immediately emptied into the press in order to damage the grapes the least possible [Figure 4.13]. The scene in Paheri's tomb [Figure 4.6] might suggest that the distance travelled was short as the vineyard and the press where the contents of the baskets were emptied appear to be close to each other, and this would minimise the problem of damaging the fruit. This was also the way in which grapes were harvest in the south of Europe until the 20th century.

Nonetheless, we do not know whether ancient Egyptians used to separate the seeds from the stalk and whether they removed the rotten grapes before throwing them in the press with the rest.

❈ **Counting the baskets**

Scribes kept count of the filled baskets and wrote the total, as one can see represented in the tomb of Amenemhat [Figure 4.12] from the 12th Dynasty. Similarly, in Catalonia up to the beginning of the 20th century the date of harvest, the name of the vineyard and the total of full baskets were mentioned in the harvest records (Raventós, 1911).

II.4.2. WINEMAKING

Winemaking is documented in tomb paintings and reliefs in Egypt since the Old Kingdom period. The procedure consists of the following recorded parts:

❈ **Transporting grapes to a press**

Once workers had picked the grapes and put them in baskets, the baskets full of grapes were transported carefully to the press, as we can see in the tomb of Paheri at el-Kab [Figure 4.6]. The press was a deposit, where a group of standing men treaded grapes.

Figure 4.9. From left to right: a man waters a vine while others are busy gathering grapes; grapes are then treaded and finally further pressed in the sack press. Ptahhotep's tomb in Saqqara, 6th Dynasty, Old Kingdom (Davies, 1900). Courtesy of the Egypt Exploration Society.

Figure 4.10. Harvest and winemaking scene. Upper part: grape harvest and foot press. Middle part: sack press and men filling wine jars while a scribe registers it. Lower part: traps to hunt birds. Tomb of Khety [num. 17] in Beni Hassan, 11th Dynasty, Middle Kingdom (Newberry, 1894). Courtesy of the Egypt Exploration Society.

Figure 4.11. Harvest final scene depicting a sack press and traps to catch birds; the rest is damaged. To the left, we observe a heating and filtration process of a liquid through a fabric, that could be a unique representation of the elaboration of *Shedeh*. Tomb of Baqet [num. 15] in Beni Hassan, 11th Dynasty, Middle Kingdom (Newberry, 1894). Courtesy of the Egypt Exploration Society.

Figure 4.12. Harvest and winemaking scene. Upper part: grapes are gathered, pressed in a vat and further pressed in a sack press. Beside, grape baskets are being counted and a scribe records the total amount. Lower part: amphorae are filled up and sealed while a supervisor controls it. On the right-hand side, goats are grazing the vineyard. Tomb of Amenemhat [num. 2] in Beni Hassan, 12th Dynasty, Middle Kingdom (Newberry, 1893). Courtesy of the Egypt Exploration Society.

Figure 4.13. Grape harvest. A standing man supervises the job of labourers and tastes the grapes. Tomb of Intef [TT 155] in Dra Abu el-Naga, Western Thebes, 18th Dynasty, New Kingdom (Säve-Söderbergh, 1957). Copyright: Griffith Institute, University of Oxford.

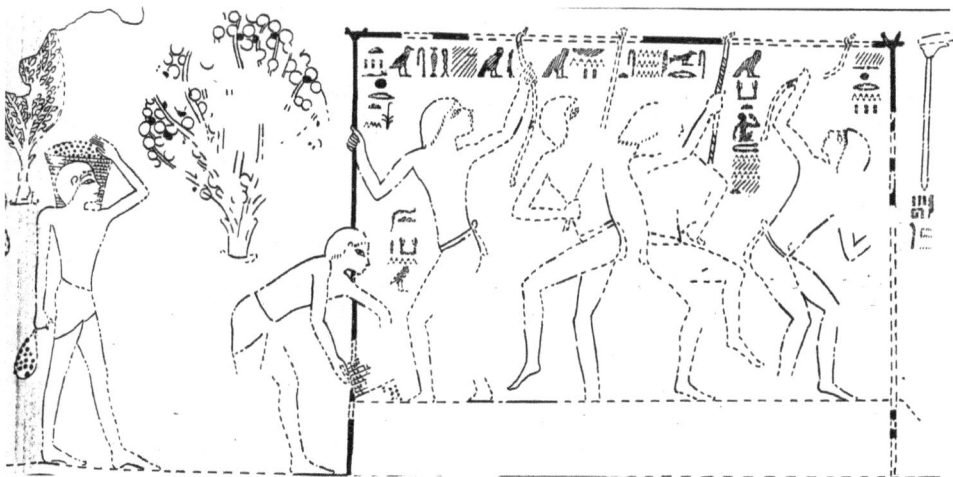

Figure 4.14. Workers empty the baskets filled with grapes into the press where a group of men tied to ropes, tread the grapes while dancing. Tomb of Intef [TT 155] in Dra Abu el-Naga, Western Thebes, 18th Dynasty, New Kingdom (Säve-Söderbergh, 1957). Copyright: Griffith Institute, University of Oxford.

Figure 4.15. Goddess Hathor, Lady of Thebes, carries an offering with grapes, among others. Nakht's Tomb [TT 52] in Sheikh Abd el-Qurna, Western Thebes, 18th Dynasty, New Kingdom.

✠ Pressing grapes

It involved treading grapes in order to extract juice from them. This element, together with the grape harvest, is always depicted in viticulture and oenology scenes of Egyptian tombs.

During the Old Kingdom [2.575-2.150 BC] and Middle Kigdom [1.975-1.640 BC] periods, the press was shallow and it is unknown whether the base of the press was round, square or rectangular (Lerstrup, 1992). On each side of the press, there was a pole or a column connected on the top by a bar that was used by the treaders to hold themselves. Treaders were a group of four to six barefoot men. And they were usually all represented in one or two lines, although this

could very well be an artistic convention more than a real procedure. In a period when machinery was not yet available, treading grapes with their bare feet was obviously a delicate operation. They held each other's waist with one hand while with the other they gripped the wooden bar above them, as we can verify it in Ptahhotep's tomb [Figure 4.9] as well as in the tombs of Niankhkhnum and Khnumhotep (Moussa and Altenmüller, 1977) both in Saqqara dating from the Old Kingdom.

Treaders could also clasp ropes that were suspended from a wooden structure supported by columns, in order not to lose balance while inhaling the aroma coming from the pressed grapes. This is depicted in the tombs of Paheri [Figure 4.6], Intef [Figure 4.14], Nakht [Figure 4.5] and Khaemwaset (Wilson, 2001) all of them located in the Theban necropolis.

According to Lerstrup (1992), during the New Kingdom period three types of press are documented. A similar press to the one mentioned above, with the only difference that ropes were hanging from the bar, for men to get hold of them. A second type was a press with poles in the shape of papyruses and a higher, rounded base with a hole through which the must, or grape juice, would flow into a vat. The tomb of Nakht illustrates it [Figure 4.5]. The third kind of press was built on a raised platform, as can be seen in Paheri's tomb [Figure 4.6]. The representation of these three types of press does not follow a chronological order as all of them can be found in Theban tombs from the 18th Dynasty until the 20th Dynasty (Lerstrup, 1992).

There is no archaeological evidence of what kind of material presses were made of (Lerstrup, 1992). While some authors believe they were made of either wood or mud, others consider stone as a more valid possibility.

It is not known what the treatment of the must was, but in the tomb of Nakht [Figure 4.5] one can see how the must, which was streaming out of the press through a pipe into a container located below, had a reddish colour. It would, in fact, take some time in contact with the skin to get that colour. It is the so called pellicular maceration or steeping of grape skins in must to extract colour avoiding vegetable and earth sediments during fermentation.

In some scenes we see how, while a group of men were treading grapes, two seating officials established a work rhythm by beating two sticks, as it was recorded during the Old Kingdom, making this repetitive job more pleasant. Treaders would sing and dance while they worked, as depicted in the tomb of Intef [Figure 4.14]. Even in modern-day Egypt, one can hear people singing while performing repetitive jobs like, for example, carrying a stone block to rebuild an old temple.

⚜ **Pressing the remains in a sack press**

After treading the grapes, the remains of skin and stones were pressed in a sack press. The pulp was put in a bag that had two sticks attached to the ends to enable it to be twisted. Two groups of men, one on each side, were using force to turn them in opposite directions in order to squeeze it and obtain a more concentrated amount of must.

Images of the sack press are found in Old Kingdom tombs such as Pepiankh's in Meir [Figure 4.3], Niankhkhnum's, Khnumhotep's (Moussa and Altenmüller, 1977) and Ptahhotep's [Figure 4.9] all three tombs in Saqqara. During the Middle Kingdom it was also portrayed in the tomb of Khety [Figure 4.10] and in the tomb of Amenemhat [Figure 4.12], both in Beni Hassan. The sack press is always represented together with the foot press. We can find the foot press represented on its own in complete scenes, but not the sack one.

Either one of the two bars used to screw was attached, as it can be seen at Baqet's tomb [Figure 4.11] in Beni Hassan, or both of them were, as shown in the tomb of Intef [Figure 4.17] from a posterior date, the New Kingdom. The last way made the operation easier and less people were needed. This could have been an evolution.

Sack press was not much depicted during the New Kingdom but this fact does not mean that it was not used anymore, because it is found in at least two Theban tombs: that of Ineni [TT 80] and that of Intef [TT 155], as previously mentioned.

This kind of press could be compared to a turbine used to further squeeze grapes using a centrifugal force. The resulting must would have had colour because of its contact with the broken skins during the pressing process. There are no records on whether the two kinds of must obtained from the two different presses were mixed afterwards.

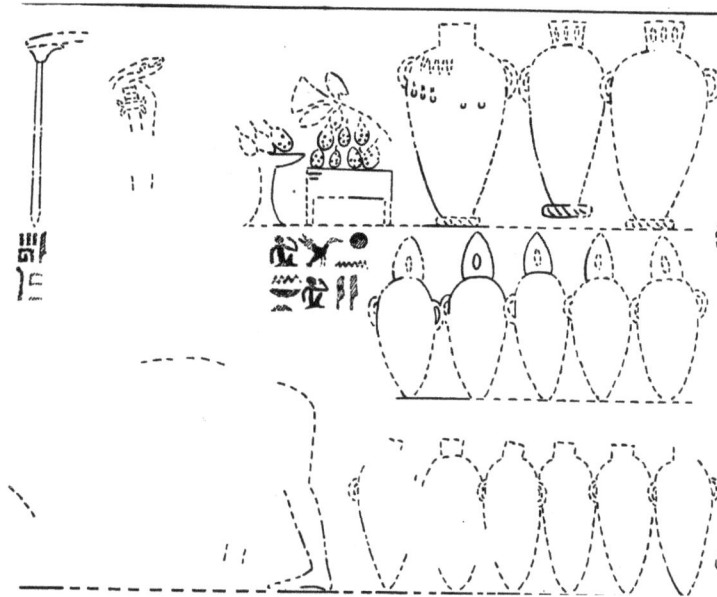

Figure 4.16. On the right-hand side, some amphorae are filled with fermenting must while others are already sealed. On the left-hand side, goddess Renenutet dominates the winemaking scene. Tomb of Intef [TT 155] in Dra Abu el-Naga, Western Thebes, 18th Dynasty, New Kingdom (Säve-Söderbergh, 1957). Copyright: Griffith Institute, University of Oxford.

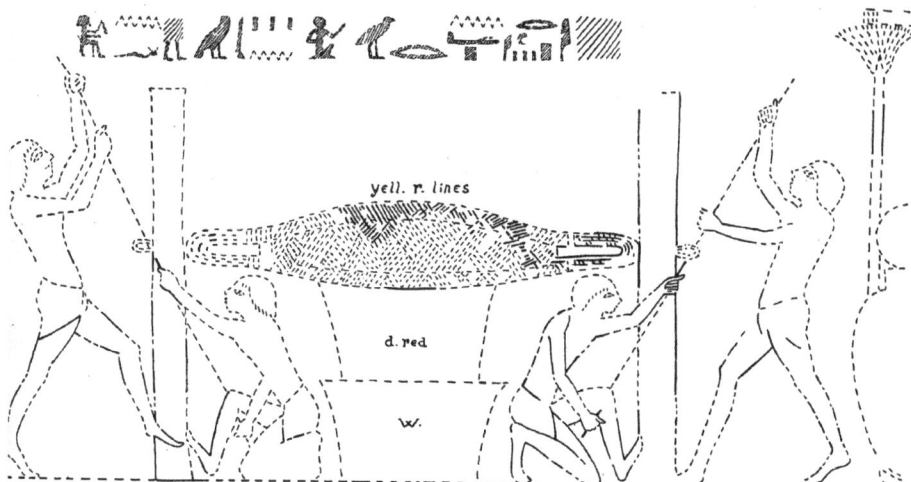

Figure 4.17. A sack press with the two attached poles. Tomb of Intef [TT 155] in Dra Abu el-Naga, Western Thebes, 18th Dynasty, New Kingdom (Säve-Söderbergh, 1957). Copyright: Griffith Institute, University of Oxford.

Some authors state that sack press could have been used to elaborate a lower-quality wine, or that the quality references writen on amphorae could refer to this difference (Lerstrup, 1992). However, nothing allows us to confirm the one or the other.

⊛ Filling wine jars

The must was collected from the press in small vases to be poured immediately after into big terracotta jugs or amphorae, where it would ferment. This scene comes after the foot press, as shown in Nakht's tomb [Figure 4.5], or after the sack press when both are represented, as it is the case in the tomb of Pepiankh in Meir [Figure 4.3] from the 6th Dynasty, and Khety's tomb [Figure 4.10] in Beni Hassan, from the Middle Kingdom.

Some authors suggested that the interior of the amphorae would have been recovered with resin, as it would later happen in ancient Greece. But an examination of the inside of Tutankhamun's amphorae carried out by Alfred Lucas (1962) did not confirm it. It seems, therefore, that the Greeks would have introduced this technique later on in Egypt (Lerstrup, 1992).

⊛ Fermentation

Fermentation took place inside amphorae, like a scene in Intef's tomb attests [Figure 4.16], where some amphorae have already the lid on. This was, without any doubt, the most important part of the process. It probably happened spontaneously because of the wild yeast adhered to grape skin.

Figure 4.18. A woman offers wine to a seated male figure who tastes it. The right scene represents the transport of amphorae to the cellar by porters who hold them by their handles. Tomb of Intef [TT 155] in Dra Abu el-Naga, Western Thebes, 18th Dynasty, New Kingdom (Säve-Söderbergh, 1957). Copyright: Griffith Institute, University of Oxford.

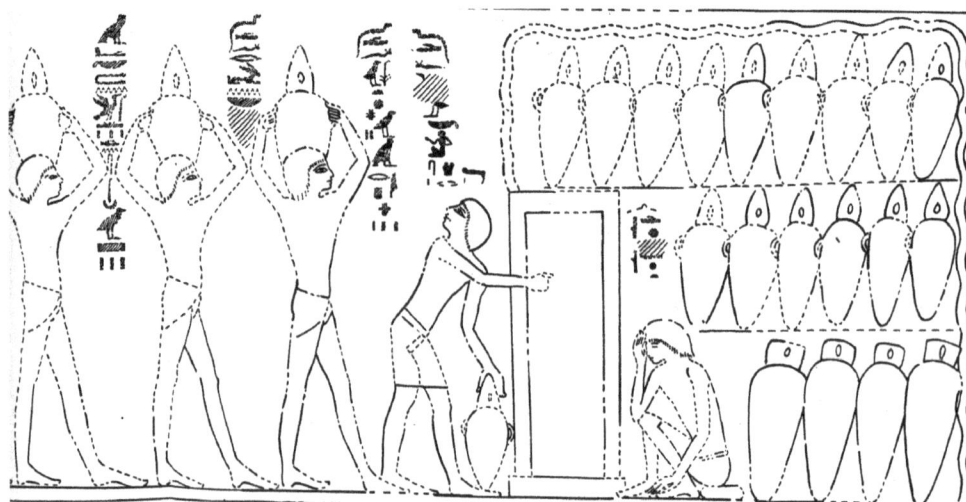

Figure 4.19. Wine vessels had two handles to be held during their transport; amphorae were then stored in a cellar. Tomb of Intef [TT 155] in Dra Abu el-Naga, Western Thebes, 18th Dynasty, New Kingdom (Säve-Söderbergh, 1957). Copyright: Griffith Institute, University of Oxford.

✠ Offerings to goddess Renenutet

During the New Kingdom, snake goddess Renenutet was related to grape harvest. In Intef's tomb [Figure 4.16] a crouching man is filling amphorae with the must coming from the press. Before him, in the upper part, there is a chapel with Renenutet to whom offerings have been made.

✠ Wine tasting

A unique scene in the tomb of Intef [Figure 4.18] represents wine tasting. It is part of a winemaking scene where a woman offers a glass of wine to an elderly man who is sitting inside a house made of papyrus saying: "For the ka! Receive the good thing with the ka from herald Intef!". This expression could be interpreted as follows: "Take this and drink to the health of herald Intef!" (Säve-Söderberg, 1957). He answers, in his turn: "How sweet this worker's wine is! For the ka of herald Intef as a gift for you, from Renenutet" (Säve-Söderberg, 1957). This man would be the oenologist responsible for winemaking and he would be tasting the wine to check whether it was good enough to be stored in the cellars to ripen (Säve-Söderberg, 1957).

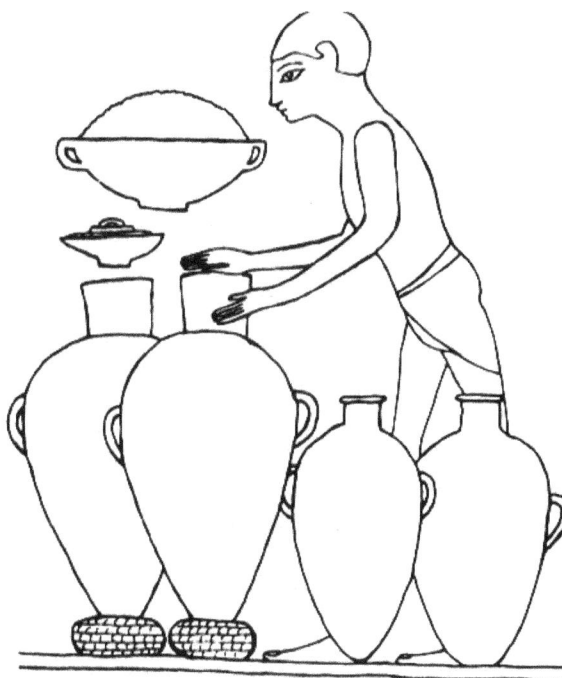

Figure 4.20. A man seals an amphorae by placing a pottery lid on its mouth. Tomb of Khaemwaset (TT 261) in Western Thebes, New Kingdom (Hope, 1993). Copyright: Griffith Institute, University of Oxford.

✠ Sealing amphorae

New Kingdom tomb scenes, like for instance the tomb of Khaemwaset [Figure 4.20], register the closure of amphorae after the fermentation process was finished. Amphorae were sealed with a lid made of reed, pottery or, less frequently, mud (Hope, 1978). A scene in the tomb of Khaemwaset [Figure 4.20] shows the way in which the lid or stopper made of pottery was placed. Then, the amphora was sealed with mud. Most of the seals had a cylindrical shape as shown on Figure 4.21, and they were mould-made or modelled into shape by hand (Hope, 1978). The main purpose of the pottery stopper would seem to have been to prevent the mud of the sealing from dropping into the amphora, because this could contaminate the wine, while the mud seal would cover the whole of the mouth and the neck of the amphora completely (Hope, 1978) to close it as hermetically as possible [Figure 4.21].

While the mud was still fresh, a seal with hieroglyphs was stamped on it indicating the name of the product and its ownership, and sometimes also its quality as shown in the tomb of Parennefer [Figure 4.22] in Western Thebes.

In the case of Tutankhamun's wine amphorae, their mud stopper was cylindrical and handmade with a seal that could be either big or small but always mentioned the name of the product and its owner. According to Hope (1993), small seals were placed on top of re-sealed holes that would have been made to release carbonic anhydride from the amphorae avoiding its rupture.

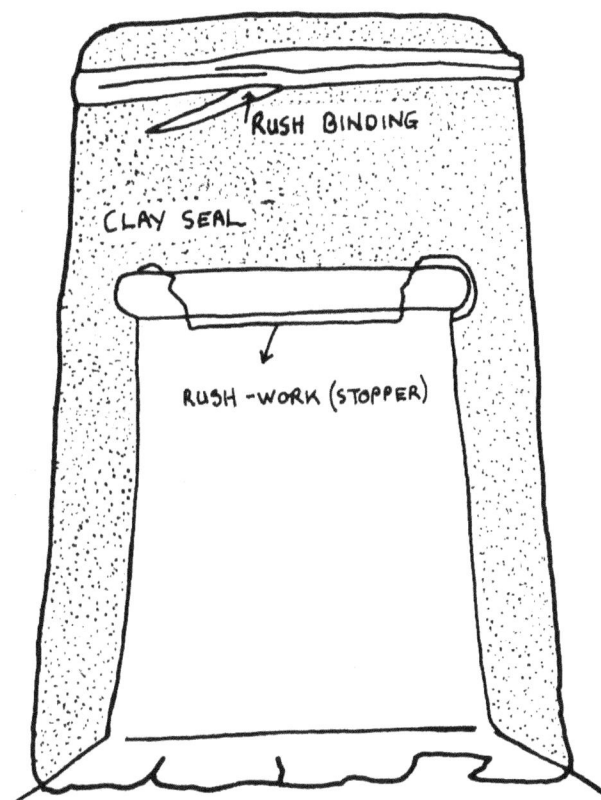

Figure 4.21. Drawing of a clay seal of a New Kingdom amphora. It is a cylindrical seal made of clay that covers the mouth and neck of the amphora entirely. Under it, one can also observe the rush stopper on top of the mouth (Hope, 1993). Copyright: Griffith Institute, University of Oxford.

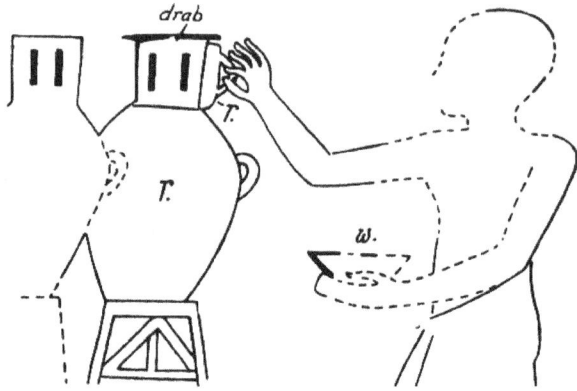

Figure 4.22. The clay seal was stamped with the name of the product and the estate where it was coming from. Tomb of Parennefer [TT 188] in Western Thebes, New Kingdom (Hope, 1993). Copyright: Griffith Institute, University of Oxford.

✵ Labelling amphorae

This activity is never depicted in tomb reliefs or paintings, although we know of its existence during the New Kingdom because hundreds of amphorae inscriptions have been found mainly in the sites of Malkata, Amenhotep III's palace in Western Thebes, in el-Amarna and also in Deir el-Medina, the worker's village in Western Thebes.

It involved writing detailed information about the harvest in hieratic [a kind of quick script] with the help of black ink on the upper part of amphorae [Figure 4.23]. Inscriptions gave the year of harvest, the name of the product, its quality, its origin, its owner and the name of the winemaker. The latter was followed by the title "chief of vintners", and he would be the scribe who wrote it. According to Tallet (1995), the seal stamped on the stopper would be previous to the inscription.

Inscriptions would be used to control the provenance of the wine and its quality once it had been sealed in a jar. This fact proves the existence of well-established criteria to assess wine as well as the existence of experts who were able to judge and evaluate the quality of wine based on its inscription in ancient Egypt (Johnson, 1989), in the same way modern Regulatory Council for Origin Denominations [Spanish D.O.] does.

Information coming from the stopper's seal was meant to make it easier to identify the contents and amphora's inscriptions would give extra data about the harvest. These inscriptions are a precursor of modern-day labels in wine-bottles.

✵ Registration

Records of the total number of amphorae were kept, as we can see at Khety's tomb in Beni Hassan [Figure 4.10], where two men are filling amphorae with wine in front of a scribe who is writing everything down. Behind him, two baskets

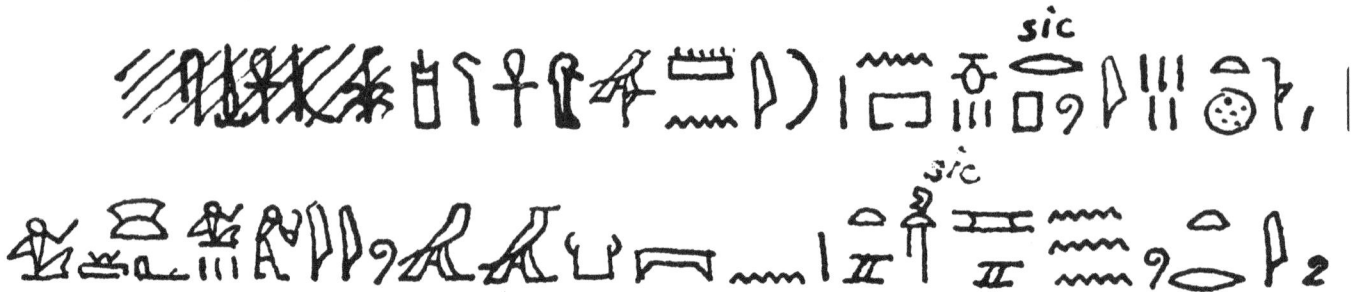

Figure 4.23. Inscription in amphora JE 62313 from Tutankhumon's collection, in the Egyptian Museum in Cairo. The upper part, written in hieratic script, reads: "Year 5, Wine from the estate of Tutankhamon, Ruler-of-Souther-On, l.p.h., [in] the Western River, chief vintner Khaa." The lower part, indicates the same inscription in hieroglyph writing (Černy, 1965). Copyright: Griffith Institute, University of Oxford.

show that he could be the same scribe who had previously counted the baskets.

✠ Transporting wine jars to a cellar

Wine jars were taken to a cellar where they were stored. They were carried one by one on porters' shoulders while held by their two side handles, in the way it is depicted in the tomb of Intef [Figures 4.18 and 4.19]. Amphorae were stored in the cellars of temples, palaces and private houses. An example of a full cellar is represented at Intef's tomb [Figure 4.19] where we can attest that amphorae were slightly tipped towards the wall (Meeks, 1993).

✠ Refrigeration during fermentation

In the hot Egyptian climate, must had to be cooled down to avoid the process of fermentation from stopping, because its sugar would not convert into alcohol then. In Paheri's tomb (Tylor and Griffith, 1894) in el-Kab, a scene shows how a worker was waving a fan to avoid the temperature rising too much inside the cellar where wine jars were kept. This act was also performed at the storerooms of the royal palace in el-Amarna, according to a relief in Parennefer's tomb [Figure 4.24] at el-Amarna.

A French traveller of the 17th Century called Vansleb recounted how this vinification method was still in use in the oasis of Fayum, Egypt, in Coptic villages (Lerstrup, 1995). Girard (1812) bore witness to the existence of this winemaking procedure at the beginning of the 19th Century.

Figure 4.24. Storeroom of the royal palace full of amphorae; men are waving fans to refresh the environment. Tomb of Parennefer at el-Amarna, Akhenaten's reign, 18th Dynasty, New Kingdom (Davies, 1908). Courtesy of the Egypt Exploration Society.

II.4.3. COLOUR AND SYMBOLISM OF WINE IN ANCIENT EGYPT

Inscribed amphorae from the New Kingdom let us know how important it was for Egyptians to have some harvest details –such as the year and the origin- at their disposal in order to select wine.

However, it is curious that no mention was made on the colour of wine, either white or red. According to Murray (2000), red wine was the most common as it is suggested by texts and visual representations.

For Montet (1913) Old kingdom and Middle Kingdom scenes represent the elaboration of red wine and, what's more, when depictions had preserved its original colour "wine and grapes were painted in dark blue". Montet (1913) affirms that he saw it at Ptahhotep's tomb in Saqqara and in other tombs in Beni Hassan [num. 2, 15 and 17]. In Nakht's tomb in Western Thebes, the must that comes out of the press is painted in dark red [Figure 4.5].

The first mention of white wine in Egypt comes from the Greco-Roman period [332 BC-395]. Athenaeus from Naucratis [2nd-3rd century BC], explains that Mareotis wine came from the area of Lake Mariut near Alexandria, and he says that this wine was "excellent, white and enjoyable, aromatic, easy to assimilate, fine and does not go to one's head apart from also being diuretic" (Athenaeus I, 33 d-f).

The second chapter of the book "Georgics" [Georgicon II, 91] written by Latin poet Virgil in the 1st century BC, between years 39-29 BC right before Egypt was assimilated by the Roman Empire, is devoted to winemaking. Virgil (1586) gives a list of vineyards highlighting Tasos' vines and white grapes from Mariut [*Sunt Thasiae vites, sunt et Mareotides albae*].

Wine symbolism is first documented in the late 5th Dynasty "Pyramid Texts" of Unis at Saqqara. Wine was used in royal funerary rites (Poo, 1986). During the ritual of the preservation of the body, five different kinds of wine were offered:

— Lower Egyptian wine, from the North.

— *abesh* wine-amphora.

— *Imt* wine coming from the Eastern Delta, Buto or maybe Pelusium.

— wine from *H3m*, exact location uncertain, maybe Western Delta.

— wine from *Snw*, maybe Pelusium.

(Faulkner, 1969: Utterances 153-157; Mercer, 1952; Poo, 1986).

In the Pyramid Texts it is said that wine can perform the ritual of the "Opening of the Mouth" to the dead (Poo, 1986).

Wine was related to red colour, the colour of the Nile during the flood caused by muddy sediments coming from the Ethiopian Blue Nile and Atbara rivers. Grape harvest and winemaking were associated to god Osiris, "the first god that came back to life" (Cherpion, 1999). The deceased were connected to the death and resurrection of Osiris (Desroches-Noblecourt and Kuenz, 1968). Mythology explains how Osiris was killed by his brother, god Set, and thrown into the Nile, where his wife Isis found him. Death was assimilated to the Nile and the re-finding of life during the flood would bring about a re-encounter with Osiris (Desroches-Noblecourt and Kuenz, 1968). Osiris' blood was identified with new wine. The ceiling of Sennefer's tomb in Western Thebes is decorated with a painted vine symbolising the rebirth of the deceased (Desroches-Noblecourt, 1985).

Grape harvest coincided with the Nile rise and flood, fact that turned grapes into a resurrection symbol still in use in Coptic iconography (Desroches-Noblecourt, 1995).

II.5. WINE AMPHORAE

The presence of actual wine jars in Egyptian tombs since the Predynastic period [4.000-3.150 BC] allow us to confirm the importance of wine for ancient Egyptians, particularly for funerary purposes as an offering to the ka -or spirit- of the dead. Since the 1st Dynasty [2.950-2.775 BC] wine jars were large in size, being more than one meter high, and they had an ideogram with the name of the vine where they came from or the royal seal -the Horus name of the king- imprinted on the mud stopper. The word for wine [*irp*] has been documented since the 2nd Dynasty [2.775-2.650 BC] (Murray, 2000).

Although no wine jars dating from the Old Kingdom or the Middle Kingdom have been found, wine must have been produced at that time if we take into account the extensive documentation concerning grape harvest and winemaking that comes from tomb paintings. According to their representations, Old Kingdom amphorae must have been pretty large and had a flat base (Meeks, 1993) as we see illustrated in the tomb of Pepiankh in Meir [Figure 4.3].

During the New Kingdom [1.543-1.078 BC] wine jars had a height of about 65 cm and, normally, two handles to facilitate its transport. A cylindrical lid of about 18 cm made of mud covered them and a seal was stamped on the lid. The seal, written in hieroglyph script, gave basic information about the product: name and place of elaboration.

In the upper and wider part of the wine jar more detailed information about the harvest could be found. This inscription consisted often of two lines written in hieratic scritp -a kind of cursive- in black ink [Figure 5.1].

Tutankhamun's amphorae have both a seal on their stopper and a hieratic inscription, proving that both labels could be placed on the same jar, fact that up to now, according to Hope (1993), had been suspected but not proved in other jars. According to Tallet (1995), the seal on the lid would be earlier than the inscription on the jar, which would be written by the person responsible for making wine at the end of the process.

Wine jars destined for the king or the most important temples were the labelled ones. According to Meeks (1993) most of the jars did not have any inscription as they contained wine that was both produced and consumed in the same place. These non-inscribed amphorae were like a table wine without Origin Denomination [D.O.] of today.

El-Amarna amphorae let us know that most wine produced during Akhenaten's reign, at the end of the 18th Dynasty, came from the West Delta, or "Western River", while the inscriptions on those coming from the Ramesseum show that during the 19th Dynasty wine came both from the East and

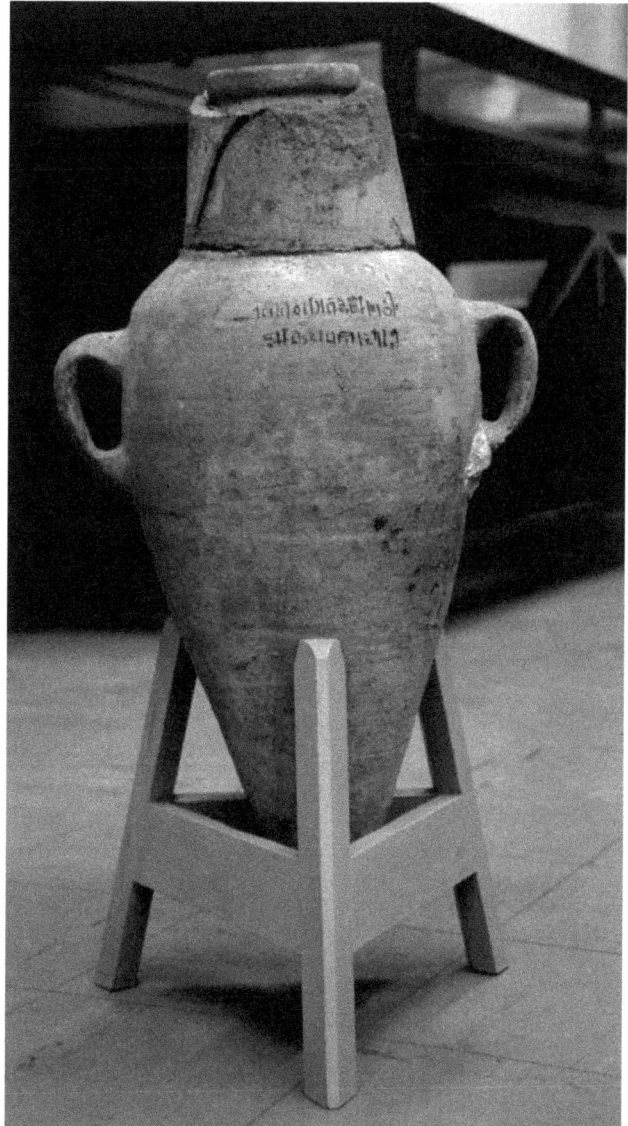

Figure 5.1. Wine jar Cairo Museum number JE 62303 found at the Annexe chamber of Tutankhamun's tomb [KV 62] at Western Thebes. The inscription reads: "Year 4, Wine from the Estate of Aten, l.p.h., in the Western River, chief vintner Nen". The clay seal is broken and it is open on its upper part. Copyright: Maria Rosa Guasch Jané, with permission from the Egyptian Museum in Cairo.

the West Delta, in a moment when the administrative capital was Pi-Ramses, located at the East Delta (Tallet, 1998).

Wine produced in private houses had no inscriptions. It was destined for personal consume and it was probably drank during the year of production, making labels unnecessary. In this way, it is not possible for us to know the real magnitude of this kind of wine, its economic impact or whether it was sold from private to private (Tallet, 1998).

In reference to wine prices, ostraca (pottery fragments with inscriptions) from the end of the New Kingdom have been found in the artisans' village of Deir el-Medina, recording that wine was between 10 and 20 times as expensive as beer

(Janssen, 1975). According to Janssen (1975), wine was not affordable by most working people because it usually came from far North and the oasis, but the court and wealthy people did consume it.

Inscriptions from New Kingdom amphorae record, in general, the following details:

▣ **The year of harvest**

The year of harvest or vintage was indicated according to the year of reign of the Pharaoh.

In the amphorae of Tutankhamun we find years 4, 5 and 9 of his reign, among them year 5 is the most cited. There is an inscription with year 10 on it but the name of the Pharaoh is not preserved, so that it is considered to belong to Akhenaten because his reign lasted for about 17 years. There is also an inscription with year 31, which can only be attributed to Amenhotep III whose reign lasted for about 39 years.

▣ **The name of the product**

The Egyptian word for wine that we find written on amphorae is properly speaking and it is transliterated as *irp* (Wörterbuch I, 1926: 115) or even *jrp*. It derived into ΗΡΠ in Coptic (Meyer, 1986; Wörterbuch I, 1926: 115).

However, during Akhenaten's reign (end of the 18th Dynasty) the inscriptions on the amphorae also mention the word *Shedeh,* whose meaning is not known for certain. Sometimes a "sweet wine" [*Irp nedjem*] is also mentioned.

In the wine jars of Tutankhamun the words wine [*Irp*], sweet wine [*Irp nedjem*] and *Shedeh* appear.

▣ **The area of production**

Most of New Kingdom wine jars came from the so-called area "Western River", the ancient Canopic branch of the Nile located at the Western Delta now disappeared.

Most of wines in Tutankhamun's tomb came from the Western River. Besides, there is a sweet wine from Qaret, possibly located at the Eastern Delta (Černy, 1965), a sweet wine form Tjel, at the North-East border of the Delta (Černy, 1965), and a very good wine which came from Iaty, the Kharga oasis (Lesko, 1977).

▣ **The name of the estate**

That was normally the property of a Pharaoh or a temple or, less often, the name of a private person.

Tutankhamun's wines were from the "Estate of Aten", in other words, they belonged to the land of Aten's Temple in the West Delta, or from the "Estate of Tutankhamun-Chief-of-South-Heliopolis", coming from the royal land of this area. Apart from them, there was an amphora with the name of vizir Pentu written on it and from which we only know that its provenance was the estate of the above mentioned vizir because no more information is added. It could be that Pentu's wine was finished up within the year and no more data was required. This wine jar would have been a gift from vizir Pentu to the Pharaoh.

▣ **The name of the winemaker**

The person responsible for the elaboration of wine holds the title "chief vintner" followed by his proper name. He would be the person in charge of handwriting all the information straight onto the amphora once this one had been filled up.

The winemaker that appears more times in Tutankhamun's amphorae is Khaa. He is the chief in four of the amphorae owned by Tutankhamun's estate and in one amphora containing Shedeh from Aten's house, all of them coming from the Western river and found inside the royal tomb. Winemaker Nen made wine and Shedeh from Aten's estate in year 4 of Tutankhamun's reign. Other winemakers are: Pinehas, Rer, Nakhtsobek, Nenia, Nebnufe, Ramose and Penamun.

▣ **The quality**

The product could be either good [nfr], very good [nfr nfr] or excellent [nfr nfr nfr].

Tutankhamun's wines are among the good and very good, and his Shedeh is always "very good".

▣ **Other information**

Sometimes only a suggestion is given in the amphora, like "offering wine" and "mixed wine" (Meeks, 1993). In Malkata inscriptions stating "wine for cellebrations" were found; this wine would have been drank during big feasts like the jubileum [Heb sed] of king Amenhotep III (Lesko, 1977). None of them mentions the place of provenance or its destination.

In this way, having all this information at hand, when a wine jar had to be selected for consumption, the person making the choice could select the most adequate and valuable from a variety of harvests and vinification procedures. At the present time, we examine labels from wine bottles in the same way.

Figure 5.2. Tutankhamun's amphorae displayed at the Egyptian Museum in Cairo. Copyright: Maria Rosa Guasch Jané, with permission of the Egyptian Museum in Cairo.

II.5.1. TUTANKHAMUN'S WINE AMPHORAE

Howard Carter (1933) reckoned that there were approximately three dozen wine jars in

Tutankhamun's tomb, see Figure 5.2, most of them found in the Annexe chamber. He verified that the wine inside them "had been dried out already for a long time" (Carter, 1933). Three of them, though, were in the actual Burial chamber between the sarcophagus and the south, west and east wall respectively.

Even though several amphorae were found broken in the Annexe, Carter (1933) observed that "there was no evidence of wine having been stolen. The breakage that occurred is more likely to have been the result of the rough handling by the thieves, when removing and stealing the contents of the adjacent stone vessels".

There are nine wine jars, two amphorae with sweet wine and three with very good *Shedeh*, all of them coming from the Estate of Aten in the Western River. One sweet wine amphora comes from the Estate of Aten in Qaret and another one from the Estate of Aten in Tjel. There are seven

Figure 5.3. Pentu had several titles during Akhenaten's reign [1.353-1.336 BC]: royal scribe, chief of the servers of Aten in Aten's Temple in Akhetaten, chief of doctors and private counsellor, among others. Lintel of the tomb of Pentu [num. 5] in el-Amarna, 18th Dynasty, New Kingdom (Davies, 1906). Courtesy of the Egypt Exploration Society.

wine jars from the Estate of Tutankhamun in the Western River. There is also very good ine from Iati from year 10, one wine jar from year 31 and another one with only the words "vizir Pentu" inscribed on it. The latter is unique because of its

inscription that refers to Pentu: ‿‿‿ , name that does not occur anywhere else. As stated by Černy (1965) the vizir could be the same person as the owner of a tomb in el-Amarna [Figure 5.3] built during Akhenaten's reign, with the name

Pentu ‿‿‿ , who could have become vizir later on, during Tutankhamun's reign.

Carter (1933) acknowledged the historical value of these amphorae because of their inscriptions. Thanks to them we know that all wine jars feature either year 4, 5 or 9 of Tutankhamun's reign, apart from two of them. One came from the harvest of year 10 and as no more information is

27

added, it cannot belong to Tutankhamun's reign but to Akhenaten's, who ruled for about 17 years. The same thing happens with the amphora from year 31; it can only be attributed to Amenhotep III who reigned for 39 years. Therefore, year 9 is considered the last harvesting year of Tutankhamun's reign and, taking into account that within the tomb's context there is no other document that provides a later date, the lenght of Tutankhamun's reign has been fixed to 9 years (Lesko, 1977).

It is thanks to these inscriptions that we know that, in general, amphorae selected for the royal tomb hailed from Aten's Estate in West Delta and that most of them, twelve to be exact, were harvested during year 5. We can deduce from this, that year 5 was the best grape harvest of his reign.

Furthermore, we can affirm that the name of god Aten was substituted for the name of god Amun in the royal titulary during year 4 at the most, as it is proven by the fact that wine jars dating from year 4 already bear the name Tutankhamun. We can also infer from wine inscriptions of year 4, 5 and 9 that the name of Aten had not yet been forbidden during Tutankhamun's government as the Properties of Aten in the Delta continued to keep this name throughout Tutankhamun's reign (Lesko, 1977).

II.6. *SHEDEH*

The meaning of the word ⟨hieroglyphs⟩ *Shedeh* is unknown. *Shedeh* is transliterated as *šdḥ* (Wörterbuch IV, 1930: p 568). According to the *Wörterbuch der Ägyptischen Sprache* (Erman and Grapow, 1930) *Shedeh* is "a beverage akin to wine, sweet and strong". According to Tallet (1995) and Murray (2000), the beverage which has the name of *Shedeh* has not yet been definitively identified.

A study of the direct sources of *Shedeh* carried out by Pierre Tallet (1995) indicates that only fifteen inscriptions on amphorae exist and ten seals on stoppers of amphorae. According to Tallet (1995), this proves its relative rarity. Among these inscriptions, eleven come from el-Amarna being most of them fragments of amphora [ostraca]. Three of them come from amphorae found in the tomb of Tutankhamun and there is one ostracon from the tomb of Maya at Saqqara. If we consider the seals, five of them come from Tutankhamun's tomb [KV 62] in Western Thebes and four were found at el-Amarna.

Strangely, despite the fact that huge amounts of inscriptions on amphorae were found at Malkata - the palace of Amenhotep III -, as well as ostraca from the Ramesseum and Deir el-Medina, all sites at Western Thebes, none of them refer to *Shedeh* (Tallet, 1995). Therefore, the context is highly limited.

The oldest mention of *Shedeh* is an inscription on a fragment of amphora which was found at el-Amarna and belongs to the reign of Akhenaten, at the end of the 18th Dynasty. The inscription reads: "year 11, *Shedeh*.... the Western River [chief vintner] Pa-Aton-em..." (Pendlebury 1933: Label num. 30, Pl LVIII; Tallet 1995, Document num. 5).

The latest *Shedeh* inscription found in an amphora comes from the tomb of Maya at Saqqara, belonging to the reign of Horemheb [1.319-1.292 BC]. Maya was chief of the treasury during Tutankhamun's reign [1.332-1.322 BC] as well as during their successors', Ay [1.322-1.319 BC] and Horemheb [1.319-1.292 BC]. Maya had a very prestigious position because he kept daily contact with the Pharaoh and had the capability to influence on political decisions (Martin, 1991). The inscription on the amphora reads: "*Shedeh nedjem*", that means sweet *Shedeh* (Van Dijk 1992: Label of amphora num. 5; Tallet 1995, Doc. 15).

In the *Lexikon der Ägyptologie* for the word "beverage" (Helck, 1977) it is written: "the *Shedeh* could be pomegranate wine", and for the word "pomegranate juice" (Brunner, 1977) it is written: "from the juice of the seeds a wine is elaborated [*šdḥ*?]." That is, in both cases it is suggested that the *Shedeh* could have been a pomegranate wine.

The hypothesis that *Shedeh* could have been elaborated with pomegranates was first suggested by Victor Loret, in 1892, in his book "La flore pharaonique". As stated by Loret (1892), Egyptian texts from the Ramessid period often mention a liquor called *Shedeh-it*. Loret (1892) refers to a text, the papyrus Anastasi IV [Anastasi IV, 6-7] that describes the production of a fruit garden of Ramses II where two kinds of fruit were grown and, from which, three liquors were made: the fruits were grapes and pomegranates, and the liquors were wine, must and *Shedeh-it*. From this text, Loret (1892) suggested: "it seems to be certain that this liquor can only be made from pomegranates, being *granadine*, pomegranate syrup or an alcoholic ferment".

In fact, pomegranate is known and cultivated in Egypt since the 18th Dynasty (Vigoroux, 1912), which coincide with the first documentation of the word *Shedeh* that appeared during the Amarna period [about 1.450 BC] at the end of the 18th Dynasty (Tallet, 1995). Tallet (1995) considers that the Old Testament, where there are many references to pomegranates and to the pomegranate tree, might have influenced the authors on the idea that *Shedeh* would have been made from pomegranates. Although not being consistent, this supposition is still found in relatively recent bibliography like the study of inscriptions and stoppers on Tutankhamun's amphorae by Hope (1993), where *Shedeh* is translated as pomegranate wine. But Tallet (1995) considers the hypothesis suggested by Loret to be weak because it was established by a simple addition of words, affirming that it is more appropiate to identify *Shedeh* with a kind of wine rather than using the translation "pomegranate wine".

Lucas (1962) suggested that *Shedeh* was a grape juice considering the inscription on the amphora at the Cairo Museum JE 62324 (Černy, 1965): "Year 4. *Shedeh* of very good quality from the Estate of Aten, l.p.h, of the Western river. Chief of vintners Nen." On the contrary, Mathieu (1996: Papyrus Harris 500 note 220, p. 75), prefers to translate *Shedeh* as liquor as he considers that "the beverage has not still been identified with certainty [pomegranate wine, date wine, cooked wine?]".

The Papyrus Salt 825 [BM 10051] is the only text found, untill now, that gives indications about the elaboration of *Shedeh*. The text, which dates from the Late period [715-332 BC], reads: "This is [...] repeat the filtration, heating again. This is the way how *Shedeh*, which Ra has given to his sons, is made" [Papyrus Salt 825 II,1] (Derchain, 1965) see Figure 6.1. Derchain (1965) studied the text and he regreted that "the raw material which is the object of this chemistry could not be known

Figure 6.1. Papyrus Salt 825 [BM 10051] in the British Museum, London, from the Late Period [715-332 BC] is the only text which describes the preparation of the *Shedeh*. Due to a damage in the papyrus on the right side below, the starting product of the *Shedeh* –its raw material- was unknown. The sentence on the top, left side, from right to left reads: "[...] repeat the filtration, heating again. This is the way how *Shedeh*, which Ra has given to his sons, is made". Copyright: Maria Rosa Guasch Jané.

because of a blank in the text." This is due to damage in the papyrus where the starting product was stated. Despite of that, the Papyrus Salt 825 provides us with the knowledge that *Shedeh* was obtained by repeated laborious operations that involved at least two filtrations and two cooking procedures (Derchain, 1965).

Moreover, the elaboration process described in the papyrus rules out certain identifications, which had been proposed, like must and grape juice (Derchain, 1965). In this way, Derchain (1965) considers that "it cannot be must or simple wine" but one "obtained from a treated fruit juice that had been filtered and cooked several times". Derchain (1965) wonders whether it could be a kind of cooked wine. In Roman times, grape juice was concentrated down by heating to obtain *defrutum*, in the same way that Malaga liqueur wines are obtained today, which are sweeter and darker than ordinary wines.

According to Gardiner (1947) *Shedeh* is "a much discussed word" and he proposes, following the *Wörterbuch* (Erman and Grapow, 1930), a beverage similar to wine, due to the fact that the word *Shedeh* appears very often next to the word *Irp*.

Even though Loret (1892) and other writers believed *Shedeh* to be pomegranate wine, Gardiner (1947) agreeing with Keimer (1924) says that there is no evidence of that. Tallet (1995) considers that there is nothing, at least within the egyptological documentation, that allows us to identify *Shedeh* with pomegranate wine, and considers that its originality would lie in its elaboration. Consequently, it would be "a liquid that, without being identical to wine, it would be at least extremely near to it" (Tallet, 1995).

Shedeh has also been discussed, to no significant conclusion in a recent work by Murray (2000).

As mentioned above, on wine inscriptions we can find the year of harvest, the area of production, the estate where it comes from and its quality in addition to the name of the winemaker. The same stands for *Shedeh*. In Tutankhamun's amphorae the production area of *Shedeh* and wine are the same, which is in this case "the Estate of Aten in the Western river", and the chief of the vintners is also the same, meaning that he would be responsible for the manufacture of both *Shedeh* (Černy, 1965: I. Wine-jars n°3, amphora JE 62.324) and *Irp* (Černy, 1965: I. Wine-jars n°2, amphora JE 62.303). For Tallet (1995), this fact would reinforce the hypothesis that both products come from grapes.

A unique scene in the tomb of Baqet at Beni Hassan [Figure 4.11] could represent the elaboration of *Shedeh*, according to Tallet (1995), because there is a heating process and, later, a filtration through a cloth.

Not only record the inscriptions that *Shedeh* was less common than wine but also a recount of fruit and products manufactured during the Ramessid

Figure 6.2. Inscription on amphora Cairo Museum number JE 62315: "Year 5, very good quality *Shedeh* from the Estate of Aten in the Western River, chief vintner Rer" being the quality "very good" emphasized on its upper part. This amphora was found by Howard Carter in between the shrine and the south wall of the Burial chamber of Tutankhamun's tomb [KV 62] at Western Thebes, and it belongs now to the collection of the Egyptian Museum in Cairo. Copyright: Griffith Institute, University of Oxford.

period –documented by Anastasi Papyrus IV [6,10-7,9]- gives a total of 1500 wine jars for 50 containing *Shedeh* (Tallet, 1998).

The word *Shedeh* appears in literary texts (moral precepts and love poetry) and juridical writings (Papyrus Harris I), in religious texts and also among the offerings represented on temple walls, mainly during the Ramessid and Ptolemaic periods (Tallet, 1995). It recurs in love poetry.

For example, in the Harris Papyrus 500 (Mathieu 1996: Papyrus Harris 500 [7,10] p 64, and note 258 p 79) a girl describes an idyllic garden with flowers where to wander with her lover and then she says to him:

"The *Shedeh* is for me like listening to your voice and I live to listen to it."

šdḥ p3y=i sḏm ḫrw=k 'nḫ=i n sḏm=f

There is plenty of documentation about the use of *Shedeh* in religious contexts during the Ptolemaic period [305-30 BC] (Tallet, 1995), coming from both religious texts and texts about embalming. At the temple of Dendera, a text refers to a "cooked wine called *Shedeh* for embalming" (Chassinat, 1968). We also find references to *Shedeh* in the Book of the Dead (Barguet, 1967). According to it, *Shedeh* would be placed near the deceased, fact that is reinforced by the existence of a *Shedeh* amphora in Tutankhamun's Burial chamber.

II.6.1. *SHEDEH* INSCRIPTIONS ON TUTANKHAMUN'S JARS

Three inscriptions on amphorae and five seals stamped on Tutankhamun's amphorae state that the product they contained was *Shedeh*. All three amphorae came from the "Estate of Aten in the Western River", being two of them from the fourth year of reign and the third one from the fifth. Four of the five stoppers were made in "Aten's Estate".

In order to realise how important the *Shedeh* amphora from Cairo Museum JE 62315 [Figure 6.2] -object of our study in the experimental section- is, we will now comment on the three *Shedeh* inscriptions on Tutankhamun's amphorae.

× **Amphora Cairo Museum num. *JE 62305*** (Černy, 1965: Wine-jars nº5 p. 1; Holthoer 1993: nº5 p. 46; Tallet 1995: Doc 13).

Lying on and among a mass of material on front of the doorway of the Annexe.

It has a stopper covering both the mouth and the neck of the amphora which had already been broken and repaired in Ancient times. This amphora is closed.

Its inscription reads: "Year 4. Very good *šdḥ* from Aten's Estate in the River [...] Chief vintner Khay."

× **Amphora Cairo Museum num. *JE 62315*** (Černy, 1965: Wine-jars nº13 p. 2; Holthoer 1993: nº13 p. 49; Tallet 1995: Doc 14).

31

Lying on the ground beside the south wall of the Burial chamber.

Traces from the stopper that according to El-Khouli (1993) it would have covered both mouth and neck, are still visible but its current location is not known. This amphora is open on its upper part. El-Khouli (1993) affirms that it contained no residues, probably following Carter's excavation notes.

The hieroglyphic inscription reads: "Very good" and below it is written in hieratic: "Year 5. Very good *šdḥ* from Aten's Estate of the Western River. By chief vintner Rer" [see Figure 6.2].

× **Amphora fragment Cairo Museum num. *JE* 62324a**

(Černy, 1965: Wine-jars nº3 p. 1; Holthoer 1993: nº3 p. 45; Tallet 1995: Doc 12).

Lying against the wall under the threshold of the doorway of the Annexe.

This amphora was broken because of the weight of stone and waste material thrown during the tomb's plunder. Only the upper part and the amphora's neck survived, apart from the stopper, which is actually intact (Hope, 1993).

The inscription reads as follows: "Year 4. Very good *šdḥ* from Aten's Estate, l.p.h., of the Western river. By chief vintner Nen."

Therefore, the amphora JE 62315 is the only complete one and open on its upper part.

II.7. PREVIOUS STUDIES

All analytical studies aimed at identifying tartaric acid in archaeological samples that had been performed up till now, used the following techniques:

a) Thin-layer chromatography and gas chromatography to identify the presence of wine. Condamin and Formenti (1976 and 1978) searched for wine traces in two Roman wine jars coming from the underwater site of Madrage de Giens, France. The samples had sediments but also a liquid part. The latter was decanted by ionic interchange column, then acidified and acid tartaric extracted with the help of ether. The results showed a "very probable" presence of tartaric acid, confirmed also by gas chromatography. Within the reddish sediments, the object of research was any substance supposedly derived from the degradation of tannins and anthocyans. A warming in an acid environment did not give conclusive results and, therefore an alkaline degradation at 300ºC during 1 hour, an acidification and a posterior extraction through ether and detection by thin-layer chromatography and gas chromatography were performed. The results showed the presence of pyrogallic, parahydroxybenzoic and 3,4-dihydroxybenzoic acids, apart from tartaric acid. A current standard wine was saturated in NaCl and ammonia and subject to the same alkaline degradation with the same resulting compounds found in the amphorae. At the end of the research, the authors wondered whether in absence of liquid it would have been possible to find substances coming from wine degradation (Condamin and Formenti, 1976).

b) High performance liquid chromatography [HPLC] and gas chromatography.

Para and Riviere (1982) carried out research on the existence of phenolic and tartaric acids in samples from Roman amphorae Dressel B1 from the site Madrage de Giens, dated from the 1st century BC. The results were compared to modern wine. In order to identify tartaric acid, an extraction and alkaline fusion using gas chromatography were performed because they considered that tartaric acid did not absorb UV. A blank coming from an amphora's handle from Giens and a modern wine were used as reference samples. An alkaline oxidation of a sample of 1g was performed and the following acids were identified: protocatequic, parahydroxybenzoic, gallic and vanillic.

c) Diffuse-reflectance Fourier transform infrared spectroscopy [DRIFT].

A research on amphorae brought Badler *et al* (1990) and Michel *et al* (1993) to analyse samples from three amphora fragments coming from Godin Tepe in Iran, and Gebel Adda in Nubia [Egypt]. One of them had a dark red patch on the inside. The researchers assumed that, because of the production and consumption of wine in Godin Tepe, the amphorae subject to study would have contained wine. The Egyptian amphora from Gebel Adda in Nubia, dating from the 4th to the 6th century, was used, according to the authors, as a reference sample to be compared to other amphorae coming from "less controlled" archaeological sites such as Godin Tepe. Fragments from 3x5 cm were dipped in 250 ml of boiling acetone that was evaporated and turned into 6-7 mg of resinous solid. This solid extract was mixed with dust from KBr and the analysis was carried out by DRIFT technique.

d) The DRIFT and HPLC techniques were used to study an amphora from the Neolithic period (Mc Govern et al, 1996) coming from Hari Firuz Tepe, in Iran. In a yellowish sample of ~4 mg, the calcium salt contained in tartaric acid was identified by DRIFT and confirmed by HPLC with a silica column of 25 cm x 4,6 mm and UV detection. A sample of an Egyptian amphora from Malkata, dating from the 18th Dynasty, was used as reference.

To sum up, these techniques required large amounts of sample and, besides, they had the following disadvantages:

◈ Thin-layer chromatography.

The identification of tartaric acid was performed according to migration of the compound by comparing it to already-known, pure products and a gas chromatography with a sensitivity of several ppm [mg/L] was required to confirm it.

◈ Gas chromatography.

A derivation by means of a previous siliation had to be performed in order to volatilize tartaric acid, and this used to take about 4-5 hours. Identification was made in comparison with a standard.

◈ High performance liquid chromatography.

According to Para and Riviere (1982), phenolic acids were not properly separated during HPLC and they considered that this should be improved. After performing an alkaline oxidation to 1g of dust from a Roman amphora from the 1st century BC, syringic acid was not detected but other acids were identified: protocatequic, parahydroxybenzoic, vanillic and gallic, apart from tartaric acid. The above-mentioned compounds do not give colour to wine apart from syringic acid (see Experimental part II.2.2). A comparison with a modern-day wine resulted in the identification of the first three acids, but in none of the cases were they able to detect syringic acid. So as to identify syringic acid in a current red wine, Singleton (1996) used the HPLC technique. Syringic acid coming from malvidin was detected by performing an alkaline fusion of a red table wine using HPLC because malvidin is the main anthocyanin contained in red wines and it is present in mg/L [ppm] amounts.

◇ Diffuse-reflectance Fourier transform infrared spectroscopy [DRIFT].

This technique interprets spectra in bands and does not allow to separate the compounds from its matrix. The results gave hydroxil, carbonil and carboxylic acid groups that were interpreted as belonging to tartaric acid.

Due to the lack of an analytical method intended for archaeological samples coming from vinification that could allow us to carry out this research, and with the aim of improving and completing analysis techniques in general, a new highly sensitive method that would allow to work with small amounts of sample had to be developed. This is the reason why liquid chromatography with mass spectrometry in tandem mode was selected.

II.7.1. THE LC/MS/MS TECHNIQUE

The technique selected to carry out this research combines the liquid chromatography coupled to mass spectrometry in tandem [LC/MS/MS] to obtain a high sensitivity apart from a great selectivity in analysing compounds. High sensitivity and selectivity are essential to analyse the kind of samples we are going to study, because of the small amount of sample available - only few mg in some cases-, and because of the very low concentration in which compounds are found, a level of ppb [μg/L].

The mass spectrometer is an instrument that allows the separation of charged molecules according to its mass-to-charge ratio [*m/z*] and permits obtaining information about molecular mass and the fragmentation pattern of the compound, that is to say, the structure and the print of the molecule.

The mass spectrometer consists of three parts: an ionisation source, a mass analyser and a detector for ions.

▫ The ionisation source generates ions from the compounds that are going to be analysed, turning the compounds of the sample into ionised molecules. In this research an electrospray font has been used, which is an atmospheric pressure ionisation [API] source, where an eluent on its mobile phase is nebulised at the end of the liquid chromatography through the action of a nebuliser gas [N_2] that runs concentrically to the eluent of the HPLC. The ionisation source employed in this study presents a scheme with a hot gas current that crashes against the nebulised current at 90º and causes a turbulence zone that helps desolvatation of ions. The liquid coming from the chromatograph reaches the electrospray font through a metallic capillary to which 3000-4000 V are applied. It is here where the ions on its liquid phase take form. Repulsive forces between ions of the same charge cause their expultion through a capillary hole to a mass analiser.

▫ The mass analiser analyses ions, separates them from the analyte according to their mass-to-charge ratio [*m/z*] by means of applying voltage and radio frequencies.

Due to the kind of compounds we need to identify, ions will be negatively charged [anion] and, therefore, it will be necessary to work with negative polarity. We will use a quadrupole analiser consisting of four parallel bars shaped into a square through which ions will run. Ions are directed towards the underneath part of the square whose bars are disposed depending on the voltage applied that generates electromagnetic fields, and the mass-to-charge ratio that can go through the filter in a given moment will be determined.

▫ The detector system reproduces the sign of each ion.

III. EXPERIMENTAL PART

III.1. THE SAMPLING

As regards archaeological material, finding a complete amphora with an inscription indicating its content and moreover, actually containing residues, is really exceptional. In general, what has been found in New Kingdom sites throughout Egypt are fragments, sometimes with inscriptions.

During this research, we have worked with two different kinds of archaeological samples: the first one we will call them "pottery scratches", which are the result of literally scratching the inside of amphorae that did not carry any visible residue. And the second kind of samples are dry residue coming from the interior of amphorae. Taking into account the exceptional character of archaeological artefacts, their scarcity and how rare it is that they have survived the passage of time in a good state of preservation, it is needless to say that the amount of sample that can be destined for destructive chemical analysis is very small.

The samples under study here belong to the permanent collections of two national museums; fact that made obtaining permissions a necessary requirement to examine the objects and to gather samples afterwards.

III.1.1. AUTHORISATION FOR SAMPLING

First of all, we asked for a special authorisation from the Supreme Council of Antiquities in Egypt to be able to study wine jars from the Egyptian Museum in Cairo. Once the amphorae of our interest were identified, permission was asked to collect a minimum amount of sample residue from the inside of each of them. A total of nine samples collected from amphorae housed in the Cairo Museum have been used in this research. They belong to two different departments: Section 1, which includes Tutankhamun's collection, and Section 4 that deals with the Amarna period. Amphorae are listed according to their entry number: *Journal d'Entrée* [JE] of the Cairo Museum.

Secondly, we were given authorisation to examine some wine jars from the Department of Ancient Egypt and Sudan, in the British Museum in London (United Kingdom). A special permission was granted to collect a small amount of residue from the jars that were going to be the subject of our study. Due to the fact that none of the amphorae contained any visible residue, the inner part of the pottery jar had to be scratched to gather samples. A total of three samples coming from this museum are included in this work, listed *Egyptian Archaeology* [EA] number from the British Museum.

The next section includes a description of the samples that are going to be analysed, together with the reference number of the museum they belong to.

III.1.2. SAMPLES FROM THE EGYPTIAN MUSEUM IN CAIRO

Nine samples from the Cairo Museum are the focus of our study: eight dry residues coming from the inner part of pottery jars that have two handles and a hieratic inscription, and a thin layer sample that was covering the inside wall of a two-handled amphorae without any inscription.

III.1.2.1. REFERENCE NUMBERS OF TUTANKHAMUN'S COLLECTION

According to the catalogue of the Egyptian Museum in Cairo, the reference numbers for Tutankhamun's objects are the following:

JE= number of *Journal d'Entrée*
C= number of Carter, Excavation number or Object number
G= *Guide* number or *Exhibition* number
SR= number of the *Special Register*

We were confronted with the fact that these four registration numbers of Tutankhamun's amphorae indicated by Černy (1965) and Holthoer (1993) were confusing; some of them were missing, others were just wrong. That is why we decided to follow the catalogue of the Egyptian Museum during sampling. Considering that no SR number was published by Černy (1965) and, furthermore, Holthoer's (1993) JE, G and SR numbers are full of mistakes, we will include all these numbers revised.

The data about the amphora, position when found in the tomb as well as marks or seals come from Holthoer's work (1993) and the translation of the inscriptions are published by Černy (1965).

The amphorae are included in the:

– *Journal d'Entrée* volume XIII.
– *Special Register* volume I.

We chose the Egyptian Museum JE number as a reference number for the amphorae because it is the only one written on the objects. When sampling, we had to verify that the JE number was the one written on the amphora and that the inscription corresponded to it. In this way, the JE became the main reference of the residue samples.

In the following list, the SR number is included because it is taken from the *Special Register* book with which the curator-in-chief of Section 1 worked when sampling at the Museum.

III.1.2.2. SAMPLES FROM TUTANKHAMUN'S AMPHORAS

Eight amphorae from section 1 of the Egyptian Museum in Cairo found by Howard Carter and lord Carnarvon in 1922 in Tutankhamun's tomb [KV 62] at the Valley of Kings, in Western Thebes.

These eight amphoras were all open on their upper part as their mud stopper had been already broken or lost when the tomb was discovered.

For samples 6, 7 and 8 we follow Černy's (1965) JE, C and G numbers which were correct; note that Holthoer's (1993) JE number for sample 7 is confusing.

According to Holthoer (1993), the archaeological letters of Carter stated that no residues were detected inside most of Tutankhamun's amphorae [num. 1,2] that we are going to study, but surprisingly when we examined them, dry deposits or residues were found. Only contents of amphora number 4 were stated as "dried lees" by Carter (Holthoer, 1993).

We have added a comment on the object, the position of the object when it was found, the inscription and mark (if any), as well as the appearance of each sample at the end of the description.

On the inscriptions we will translate "house" [*pr*] by "estate" because, according to Hope (1993), it would literally mean "house" in English but here it has more the meaning of "estate".

A recurring formula in Egyptian inscriptions is also found here: life, prosperity and health [l.p.h.].

Amphorae from Section 1, Tutankhamun's collection:

1. **Amphora JE 62.301** [C=523/ G=1678/ SR=92]

   Amphora with two handles and the clay seal is missing.

   Position: Found on the ground of the Annexe chamber, near the west wall corner.

   Inscription: "Year 5. Wine of the Estate of Aten of the Western River. Chief vintner Pinehas".

   Sample: Dry residue of a light yellowish colour.

2. **Amphora JE 62.302** [C=490/ G=1679/ SR=84]

   Amphora with two handles, it has traces of a clay seal that would have covered both its mouth and neck, now missing.

   Position: Found on the ground of the Annexe chamber, next to the northern wall.

Inscription: "Vizier Pentu."

Mark in charcoal on one side:

Sample: Dry residue of a light brown colour.

3. **Amphora JE 62.303** [C=486/ G=1680/ SR=85]

   Amphora with two handles and a lid that covers its neck. Broken on its upper part [Figure 5.1].

   Position: Found on the ground of the Annexe chamber, next to the east wall.

   Inscription: "Year 4. Wine of the Estate of Aten, l.p.h., of the Western River. Chief vintner Nen."

   According to Carter the stopper would have had stamped: "Wine from Aten's Estate" (Holthoer, 1993).

   Sample: Dry residue of a light brown-yellowish colour.

4. **Fragment of amphora JE 62.312** [C=509/ G=1686/ SR=110]

   Fragment of amphora with two handles. Its bottom part is missing and its broken clay seal covers mouth and neck of the amphora.

   Position: Found lying on the ground in the middle of the Annexe chamber.

   Inscription: "Year 5. Sweet wine of the Estate of Aten of the Western River. Chief vintner Nakht."

   Mark in charcoal below the hieratic inscription:

   Seal on the stopper: on the side and on its upper part but it has not been identified.

   Sample: Dry residue of a light brown colour.

5. **Amphora JE 62.313** [C=508/ G=1687/ SR=91]

   Amphora with two handles and a broken clay seal that covers mouth and neck.

   Position: Found on the ground of the Annexe chamber, buried under waste material, near the north-west corner.

   Inscription: "Year 5. Wine from the Estate of Tutankhamun, ruler of Southern On, l.p.h., [in] the Western River. Chief vintner Khaa."

   Mark in charcoal next to the inscription: not clear.

Seal on the stopper: "Wine from Tutankhamun's Estate".

Sample: Dry residue of a dark brown colour.

6. **Amphora JE 62.314** [C=195 /G=503 /SR=106]

Amphora with two vertical handles. It has traces of a clay seal that would have covered its mouth and neck.

Position: Found on the ground of the Burial chamber, next to the west wall, between the shrines and the wall.

Inscription: "Year 9. Wine of the Estate of Aten of the Western River. Chief vintner Sennufe."

Seal in the handle: "Aten's Estate".

Sample: Dry and blackish residue.

7. **Amphora JE 62.315** [C=206 /G=502 /SR=103]

Amphora with two handles, and traces of a clay seal that would have covered its mouth and neck.

Position: Found on the ground of the Burial chamber, next to the south wall.

Inscription: "Year 5. *Shedeh* of very good quality of the Estate of Aten of the Western River. Chief vintner Rer."

Up to the inscription is emphasised: "Very good".

According to Hope (1993), the lid belonging to this amphora would have had two seals: a big one stating: "very good quality *Shedeh* from Aten's Estate" and a smaller one saying: "Wine from Aten's Estate".

Sample: Dry residue of a black colour.

8. **Amphora JE 62.316** [C=180/ G=504 /SR=99]

Amphora with two vertical handles and a missing clay seal.

Position: Found on the ground of the Burial Chamber, next to the east wall.

Inscription: "Year 5. Wine from the Estate of Tutankhamun, Ruler of the Southern On in the Western River. Chief vintner Khaa."

The handle has an inscription: "Ruler's Estate", and it refers to the king's property.

Sample: Dry residue of a light brown colour.

III.1.2.3. OTHER SAMPLES

Amphorae from Section 2 of the Egyptian Museum, in Cairo:

9. **Amphora JE 57.356**

Amphora with two handles, no lid and no inscription.

It comes from el-Amarna, from the end of the 18th Dynasty [second half of the 14th century BC].

Sample: a thin film of residue was covering the inner part of the wine jar.

III.1.3. SAMPLES FROM THE BRITISH MUSEUM IN LONDON

The Department of Ancient Egypt and Sudan from the British Museum in London provided three samples that were obtained by scratching the inside of the pottery jars because no visible residue had been preserved.

A description of these amphorae together with their date, whether they carry an inscription or not, and how the sample was obtained is provided below. Their numeration is *Egyptian Archaeology* [EA] from the Department of Ancient Egypt and Sudan, British Museum.

10. **Fragment of wine jar EA 32.684**

Fragment of wine jar. It was probably a long amphora without handles, typical of the Tinite Period. It comes from King Semerkhet's tomb in Abydos, 1st Dynasty [3.150-2.900 BC]. The preserved fragment bears an ideogram that would correspond to the name of King Semerkhet's vineyard.

Sample: It was obtained by scratching the inner part of the fragment.

11. **Jar EA 51.187**

Object catalogued as a pink jar. No inscription is written on it.

It comes from tomb 5 of cemetery 3 in Faras, Nubia [Sudan] and it dates from the beginning of the Dynastic period.

Sample: It was obtained by scratching the inside of the amphora.

12. **Wine jar EA 59.774**

Decorated amphora with a painted pottery lid and no handles. It has an inscription and it dates from the end of the 18th Dynasty or the beginning of the 19th. Unknown provenance, although el-Amarna has been suggested (Lesko, 1977).

Inscription: "Wine from the Delta for Osiris Nedkhmet".

Sample: It was obtained by scratching the inside of the amphora.

III.1.4. REFERENCE SAMPLES

Reference samples include: a blank to be compared with the samples obtained by scratching pottery jars in order to identify tartaric acid; a modern-day red and white wine, to test the presence of malvidin by releasing syringic acid; the standard of tartaric and syringic acid.

◆ **Blank of pottery**

A Fragment of an Egyptian pottery handle was scratched on one side to compare the results with the samples. It was treated on the same way as the samples to identify its tartaric acid content.

◆ **Modern wines**

We performed the oxidation of a red wine of the monovarietal Cabernet Sauvignon from D.O. Penedès (Catalonia, Spain) and a white wine of the monovarietal Xarel·lo also from D.O. Penedès.

The procedure was exactly the same one carried out with the archaeological samples. The objective was to verify whether there was an increase in syringic acid levels after the oxidation of red wine as this would confirm the presence of malvidin and corroborate that this does not happen with white wine.

◆ **Standards**

Tartaric acid standard: standard mother solution of 100 ppm prepared in 100% water; working solution of 100 μg/L made by diluting the standard solutions with the LC mobile phase [0,1% formic acid in water/acetonitrile, 90:10].

Syringic acid standard: standard mother solution of 100 μg/L prepared at a concentration of 20% methanol and 80% water; working solution of 100 μg/L made by diluting the standard solutions with the LC mobile phase [0,1% formic acid in water/acetonitrile, 90:10].

III.2. THE MARKERS

The analytical method that is about to be developed needs to allow the identification of two compounds as markers: tartaric acid as a wine marker and syringic acid as a red wine marker.

III.2.1. THE WINE MARKER

Tartaric acid is an organic acid that occurs in nature generally in large amounts [ppm] but only in grapes of the Mediterranean area and Middle East.

Tartaric acid is an established wine marker in archaeology because it can be preserved in contact with pottery being absorbed on silicates by hydrogen bonding (Michel, 1993). For that reason it can be found both in deposit residues and in residues that have been scratched of pottery. Nevertheless, it should be considered that in the second case the amounts of tartaric acid will be very low [ppb].

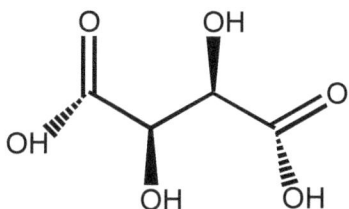

Tartaric acid (PM=150)

Tartaric acid provides no information about the colour of grapes. Accordingly, another compound needs to be established as a red wine marker.

III.2.2. THE RED WINE MARKER

Syringic acid is an organic acid that occurs free in many plants and, consequently, not particularly in grapes. According to Singleton (1996), syringic acid could be a potential red wine marker because malvidin is present in red grapes and, therefore, the syringic acid used as a red wine marker would not be free but released by malvidin.

Malvidin is a phenol of the flavonoid type with a diphenylpropanoid chain [C_6-C_3-C_6] in which the three carbons between the two phenol groups are cycled with oxygen. Malvidin [malvidin-3-glucoside] is the main anthocyanidin responsible for the colour of red grapes and the main anthocyanidin in red wine, while it does not appear in white grapes.

The structural instability of anthocyanidins affects the colour of wine in the course of time (Fulcrand et al, 1998). Molecules turn gradually into polymeric pigments with age; this explains the colour change of red wine due to the relative contribution of polymeric and monomeric pigments to the total colour (Somers, 1966). During vitification and aging processes, wine colour evolves because of progressive changes in phenolic compounds coming from grapes (Mateus *et al*, 2002). Malvidin polymerises with phenolic compounds, mostly catequines and proanthocyanidins, but also with non-phenolic ones such as acetaldehyde and pyruvic acid that occur in wine (Mateus *et al*, 2002; Atanasova *et al* 2002; Fucrand *et al*, 1998). They create more stable pigments but of difficult identification.

Studies carried out with aged wine confirm that anthocyanidins are unstable and react with other compounds during the aging process. Malvidin is the predominant anthocyanidin in young red wines and, as time goes by, it forms more stable complexes because of its interaction with other phenolic compounds that occur in wines (Mateus *et al*, 2002).

It is difficult to isolate and identify this pigment, most of all because it is found in far smaller amounts than free anthocyanidins. (Mateus *et al*, 2002). Nevertheless, it has been proven that the cycloaddition of pyruvic acid to malvidin gives more stable pigments (Bakker *et al*, 1997; Fulcrand *et al*, 1998), and that malvidin in an oxygenated environment reacts with acetaldehid creating polymers. This would partly explain the colour change and the decrease of astringents during the aging process of red wines (Atanasova *et al*, 2002).

It is not yet known what happens to these compounds and polymers formed throughout thousands of years. Singleton (1996) suggested fragmenting the polymeric structures of malvidin by means of an alkaline reaction. He put it into practice with a red table wine and he attested that syringic acid coming from malvidin was released. In the context of archaeological samples this fragmentation of polymeric structures would allow us to affirm that that wine had been made of red grapes. In this way, we will perform an alkaline oxidation in order to break the structure of the polymer and obtain syringic acid, as we can see in Figure A.

It is important to bear in mind that the presence of polymers can be very low in an archaeological residue sample.

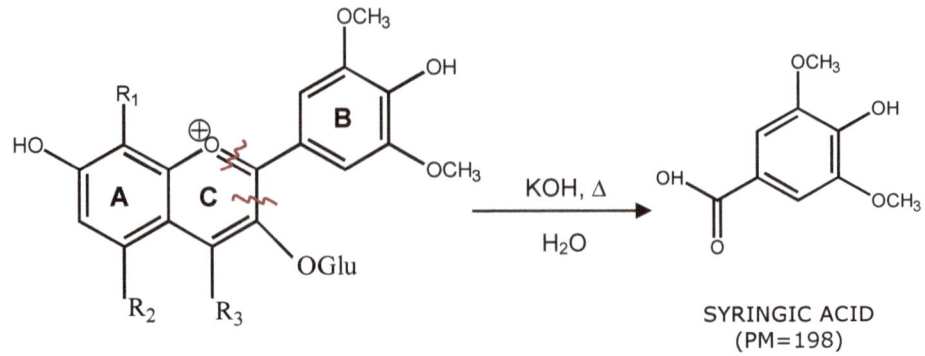

MALVIDIN-3-GLU
in the polymerized pigment

R1, R2, R3=polymeric fragments

SYRINGIC ACID
(PM=198)

Figure A: Production of syringic acid. Syringic acid is released from the flavilium structure of malvidin-3-glucoside in the polymerized pigment by alkaline fusion through the formation of a hydrated hemichemical form in which the pyran (C ring) is broken in two steps.

III.3. SAMPLE TREATMENT

We will proceed now to describe how the sample was prepared and the oxidation performed.

III.3.1. SAMPLE PREPARATION

An amount of ~2 mg of sample is weighed and put into a centrifuge tube. In order to obtain an extract, 1 ml of water MilliQ is added at about 40ºC and mixed with magnetic stirring during 2 min. Next, 4 ml of ethanol are added to the 0,1% of formic acid, and the mixture undergoes magnetic stirring during 3 min, procedure that is repeated three times. Then, it is centrifugated during 15 min at 1620 g [3000 rpm] at 10ºC to isolate two phases. The resulting supernatant is collected in a graduated cylinder and concentrated under a nitrogen environment until 500µL. It is then reconstituted with mobile phase [90% of water in the 0,1% of formic acid and 10% of acetonitrile] until 1 ml. At the end, it is filtered with an Acrodisc filter 13 CR PTFE 0,45 µm from Waters and sealed in a test tube of an amber colour. The samples are kept in a refrigerator at a temperature of –20ºC.

III.3.2. OXIDATION OF THE RESIDUES

So that syringic acid derived from malvidin contained in polymers could be released, an alkaline oxidation of the residue samples was performed following the works of Zugla and Kiss (1987) and Singleton (1996), but adapting it to the specific samples 1 to 8 from Cairo Museum.

The procedure was as follows:

After undergoing the previously mentioned preparation, the residue is poured into a precipitation vessel where two lentils of KOH [~0,23 g] are added and heated at 50ºC. We leave it 5 more minutes after the lentils are melted. Once it has cooled down, 5 ml of water MilliQ are added with the help of an automatic funnel as well as ~280 µL of trifluoroacetic acid [TFA] until pH acid [2-3]. Then, 10 mL of ethyl acetate, previously decanted with water MilliQ, are placed in a decanter. The sample is added and stirred to separate the two phases. The organic phase is concentrated in a nitrogen environment until ~250 µL., filtered with an Acrodisc filter 13 CR PTFE de 0,45 µm from Waters and reconstituted by the addition of ~250 µL of mobile phase.

The results of the modern red wine confirm an increase in the syringic acid peak obtained from malvidin after oxidation. However, no increase was attested with the white wine after oxidation, confirming that white wine does not contain malvidin.

III.3.3. MATERIALS

▫ Standards: Tartaric acid from Aldrich Chemical Co. [Steinheim, Germany] and syringic acid from Fluka Chemie AG [Buchs, Switzerland].

▫ Reactives: Acetonitrile and methanol HPLC degree of SDS [Peypin, France], formic acid and ethyl acetate of 99% purity from Panreac [Barcelona, Spain]; potassium hydroxide of 85% purity, from Carlo Erba [Milan, Italy]. Ultrapure water [MilliQ] from Millipore [Bedford, MA, USA].

▫ Filter: Acrodisc 13 CR PTFE 0,45 µm from Waters [Mildford, Massachussets, USA].

III.4. THE METHOD OF ANALYSIS

The liquid chromatograph used was an Agilent 1100 [Waldbronn, Germany] with a quaternary pump and an automatic injector. A Waters Atlantis chromatograph column [Mildford, Massachusetts, USA] was selected with an inverted phase and an octadecilsilan base [150 X 2.1 mm i.d., 5μm].

The elution gradient of the mobile phase combines 0.1% formic acid in water MilliQ [A phase] and pure acetonitrile [B phase] in the following proportions: it was initially isocratic until minute 5 with 100% of solvent A; at minute 10 solvents were A/B [80:20] and a second isocratic step was performed from minute 15 to 30 with solvents A/B [50:50]. It worked at 200μL/min at room temperature and the injected volume was 15μL.

The mass spectrometer was an API 3000 triple quadrupole MS/MS System from Applied Biosystems [PE Sciex, Concord, ON, Canada], equipped with a Turbo ion spray source. The triple quadrupole consists of three quadrupoles: the first [Q1] and the third one [Q3] act as analizers while the second quadrupole [Q2] does it as a collision cell in tandem methods, and as a filter in methods that work with only Q1. Tandem mass spectrometry involves the activation of a precursor ion created in the ion source and the analyses of the fragmentation of the mass. Collision Activated Dissociation [CAD] has been used as an activation technique by which to activate ions that are then allowed to collide with an inert gas [N_2] and a potential [CE] in the collision cell [Q2]. The activation of few selected ions occurs when a particular ion that leaves Q1 is bombed with a gas causing the fragmentation of it into smaller fragments that will be analised in Q3.

As to quadrupoles:

* The first quadrupole [Q1] selects only one mass or "precursor", characteristic of the sample's analyte. Ions from the chosen mass go through a zone where they are activated and allowed to collide with a neutral gas to produce fragmented ions or "product" in the so-called Collisional Activation [CA]. When there happens to be not enough internal energy to break the chemical bridges, ions decompose and that is the process called Collisionally Activated Dissociation [CAD].

* The third quadrupole [Q3] separates ions according to their *m/z*.

Several work techniques were used to try out the new method:

— Experiments in MS:

¤ Full Scan [Q1 Scan]: it scans ions in a specific *m/z* interval and it is used both in quantitative and qualitative analyses when all analyte ions are unknown from the start.

¤ Selected Ion Monitoring [SIM]: it measures only the *m/z* values that we choose in Q1. It is significantly more sensitive than Q1 Scan but it provides information about a smaller amount of ions and no spectral information at all.

— Experiments in MS/MS:

❋ Product Ion Scan [PIS]: it involes isolating an ion in Q1, fragmenting it in the collision cell [Q2] and scaning the resulting fragments in Q3. Confirmation is made by comparing the standard of the mass spectrum in Product ion Scan with the sample's compound. It is mostly used to structurally identify significant fragmented ions for each selected precursor.

❋ Precursor Ion Scan: it scans all possible precursors in Q1 of a particular ion from Q3. It is employed to identify a compound mix of a product ion [fragment] that has a specific compound type.

❋ Multiple Reaction Monitoring [MRM]: it fixes one ion in Q1 and another one in Q3. It is the quantitative analysis experiment par excellence due to its high sensitivity and the experiment used for most of our samples. Its disadvantage when carrying out qualitative analysis is its lack of spectral information.

The results were processed by Software Analyst™.

III.4.1. METHOD VALIDATION

According to Para and Riviere (1982), all quantitative determination of amphorae is unfounded because the subject of study evolves over time. Hence, our goal is the identification of compounds not its quantification.

Following the ICH guidelines (1997), when carrying out analytical methods with identification purposes the only parameter that needs to be validated is specificity –that is, selectivity-.

◆ **SELECTIVITY**

a) Column: A phase-inverted chromatographic column with an octadecylsilyl base was chosen to get a better retention of polar compounds –tartaric acid in this case, used in an aqueous mobile phase- and to obtain an excellent peak resolution.

b) Standard infusion: A standard infusion of tartaric and syringic acid was completed in the mass spectrometer with a glass syringe taking a volume of 200 μL of the standard at a flux of 5 μL/min with negative polarity.

c) Monitoring every compound: the goal is to optimise the parameters of the ionisation source in order to attain the maximum sign possible.

➤ Full Scan: a wide range of 100-200 was picked to find the standard and obtain the spectrum of each compound.

➤ The spectrum generated by tartaric acid [M_w150] in negative mode shows a deprotonate molecule [M-H]⁻ of DP=-25 V, while that of syringic acid [M_w198], also in negative mode, shows a deprotonate molecule [M-H]⁻ of DP=-30 V.

➤ SIM: it enhances sensitivity when identifying compounds.

➤ Product Ion Scan [PIS]: used to fragment and identify sons. For tartaric acid that has a mass of M_w=150, we consider a product of *m/z* 149 scanning from 50 to 175 during 2 seconds, and for each CAD=1 and CE=-5 we can identify the father ion. So that we can see the son ions, we modify CE=-10 and CE=-15 and we obtain several ions among which the most stable is PIS=87, resulting of the loss of groups COOH and OH.

As to syringic acid of M_w=198 and considering the product 197 we obtain PIS=182 due to the loss of group CH_3.

➤ MRM: it is employed to monitor the sign produced by the breakage of the compound [Q1] and the son [Q3], each of them in its own quadrupole.

Parameters Declustering Potential [DP] and Collision Energy [CE] were enhanced for a higher sensitivity through an infusion of individual standard solution 1 mg/L at a flux of 5μL/min in the mass spectrometer. We optimised the potential of the capillary by going from 0 to 200, 5 at a time and we achieved DP=-25 V for tartaric acid, and DP=-30 V for syringic acid. To optimise the CE we went from −5 to −45 V, achieving CE=-20 V both for tartaric and for syringic acid.

While MRM for tartaric acid was established between ions *m/z* 149 and 87 with CE=-20 V for syringic acid MRM was between ions *m/z* 197 and 182 with CE=-20 V.

d) The optimal mass spectrometer parameters in the analysis of tartaric and syringic acid are the following:

✱ Voltage Spray Ions [IS]: the capillary's voltage of the electrospray, IS=-4.500 V.

✱ Focusing Potential [FP]= -200 V

✱ Entrance Potential [EP] =10 V

✱ Nebuliser Gas [NEB]: NEB=10

✱ Curtain Gas [CUR]: CUR=12 (arbitrary units).

✱ Auxiliar Gas, temperature [TEM]: nitrogen gas at a temperature of 400ºC.

✱ CAD Gas =4 (arbitrary units), the collision gas is nitrogen.

✱ Collision Cel Exit Potencial [CXP]: -15 V

Everything introduced at a flux of 6.500 cm³/min.

e) Verifying a compound's mass spectrum of the sample: sample is injected in mode PIS=149 and compared with the same experiment standard performed under the same conditions. That is, mode PIS 149 scanned from 80 to 152 and mode Full Scan between 140-160 for tartaric acid; mode PIS 197 scanned from 175 to 200 and mode Full Scan between 175-200 for syringic acid.

◆ **SENSITIVITY**: The Limit of Detection [LOD] of the method was calculated by 10 repeated injections of the standard solution with a signal/noise ratio [s/n] 3 (USP XXVIII, 2005). The limit of detection of this method in mode MRM is 0,05 ppb, with an injection volume of 15μl.

These are the limits of detection of tartaric acid for every working mode: Full Scan has got LOD=40 μg/L, SIM has LOD=10 μg/L, PIS has LOD=80 μg/L, MRM has LOD=0,05 μg/L, thus being MRM mode the most sensitive.

III.4.1.1. DEAD VOLUME OF THE COLUMN TEST

A test was carried out to establish the dead volume of the column. The purpose of it was to confirm that the tartaric acid determined with the initial chromatography, was retained at the column and did not escape with the eluent, fact that could prevent its identification. For this very reason, we started with standard solutions known for their earlier retention times than tartaric acids such as thiourea and oxalic acid. A tartaric acid solution of 2 mg/L in 100% MQ water was measured in mass spectrometer at a flux of 0,2 mg/L, and compared with a thiourea solution of 2 mg/L in 100% acetonitrile and an oxalic solution [M_w=90] of 2 mg/L in 100% MQ water.

The obtained results concluded that thiourea was the first one to be retained, with a retention time of t_R=2,2. Oxalic acid was the second one with a retention time of t_R=2,49 being tartaric acid the third one with t_R=2,75. Therefore, oxalic acid and thiourea had a higher retention time verifying that tartaric acid was retained on the column.

III.5. ANALYTICAL RESEARCH

III.5.1. IDENTIFICATION OF WINE MARKERS IN RESIDUES FROM ANCIENT EGYPTIAN VESSELS BY LIQUID CHROMATOGRAPHY WITH MASS SPECTROMETRY IN TANDEM MODE

"Reproduced with permission from Analytical Chemistry 76 (2004), Guasch-Jané MR., Ibern-Gómez M., Andrés-Lacueva C., Jáuregui O. and Lamuela-Raventós RM., "Liquid chromatography with mass spectrometry in tandem mode applied for the identification of wine markers in residues from ancient Egyptian vessels", p. 1672-1677. Copyright [2008] American Chemical Society".

A new method for the identification of tartaric acid as a wine marker in archaeological residues from Egyptian vessels using liquid chromatography with mass spectrometry in tandem mode [LC/MS/MS] is presented. Owing to the special characteristics of these samples, such as the dryness and the small quantity available for analysis, it was necessary to have a very sensitive and highly specific analytical method to detect tartaric acid at trace levels in the residues. Furthermore, an alkaline fusion was carried out to identify syringic acid -derived from malvidin- as a red wine marker in a deposit residue from a wine jar found at the tomb of king Tutankhamun. Malvidin-3-glucoside, the main anthocyanin that gives young wines their red color, polymerizes with aging into more stable pigments. However, the presence of malvidin in ancient residues can be proved by performing an alkaline fusion of the residue to release syringic acid from the pigment, which has been identified, here for the first time, by using the LC/MS/MS method revealing the red grape origin of an ancient Egyptian wine residue.

Introduction

In ancient Egypt, vines were grown throughout the country, although the best wines came from the Nile River Delta and the Western oasis. Wine was an important product, offered in funerary rituals, in temples to worship gods and consumed daily by the upper classes during meals and parties (LÄ VI, 1986). Since the Early Dynastic [2.920-2.575 BC] period, wine jars were placed in tombs as funerary meals, some of them were inscribed. From the Old Kingdom [2.700-2.200 BC] to the New Kingdom [1.543-1.078 BC] periods, tomb walls of the nobles were decorated with scenes including viticulture and wine-making. Egyptian mythology even related the red color of the Nile during flooding to the color of wine (LÄ VI, 1986). The New Kingdom wine-jars were labeled with the name of the product, the year of reign, the source of origin and even the name of the vine-grower (Černy, 1965; Martin, 1991) but they did not mention the kind of wines contained. Most of the labeled jars are now only broken fragments, but some are completely preserved. Despite that, residues from archaeological vessels have been barely investigated.

Considering the special characteristics of archaeological samples, our aim was to develop a very sensitive and highly specific method for the identification of wine markers that might be present in trace quantities. In particular, tartaric acid, rarely found in nature in sources other than grapes, has been reported as a wine marker in ancient residues and can be preserved in the pottery because it can be strongly absorbed on silicates by hydrogen bonding (Michel *et al*, 1993). Analysis of ancient samples requires a very sensitive method in order to minimize the amount of sample used (Garnier *et al*, 2002). Four analytical methods have been applied for tartaric acid determination in archaeological samples. They are: thin-layer chromatography (Condamin, 1976), gas chromatography (Condamin, 1976), diffuse-reflectance Fourier transform infrared spectroscopy (Michel *et al*, 1993; Badler *et al*, 1990; McGovern *et al*, 1996) and high performance liquid chromatography with UV detection (McGovern *et al*, 1996). However, all of them lack enough selectivity and sensitivity for the size of samples available, so an improved method was required. Liquid chromatography mass spectrometry in tandem mode [LC/MS/MS] has become an ideal technique due to its speed, sensitivity and selectivity, and a powerful tool for identification based on retention times and fragmentation patterns of the compounds during MS/MS analysis apart from low detection limits. Another important feature of triple quadrupole MS instruments is that they provide the highest sensitivity in multiple reaction monitoring [MRM] mode. When the compounds are present at trace levels or the amount of sample available is limited, an MRM assay is the method of choice because it provides the highest sensitivity in MS/MS mode. The LC/MS/MS has not been used before for the analysis of tartaric or syringic acids in archaeological residues or in any other kind of sample. In addition, this LC/MS/MS method was optimized for syringic acid detection in order to study the color of a wine residue. Malvidin is the major red wine anthocyanin (Macheix, 1990) and it polymerizes with aging. By alkaline fusion of a red wine, malvidin releases syringic acid (Singleton, 1996). In that case, syringic acid identification would indicate that a dark brown wine residue had red grape origin. Syringic acid has never been detected in any archaeological samples, even though a previous attempt was made using alkaline fusion in a Roman wine residue by HPLC-UV with no success (Para, 1982).

EXPERIMENTAL SECTION

Archaeological samples

As residues from archaeological remains are very precious, a small quantity of sample was taken from the inside of Egyptian pottery vessels for

---

Archaeological samples

Sample BM1: Fragment of a wine jar, numbered EA 32684. From 1st Dynasty [2.950-2.575 BC], found at the tomb of King Semerkhet at Abydos. Inscription: name of the royal vineyard of Semerkhet.

Sample BM2: Decorated wine jar, numbered EA 59774. From late 18th to early 19th Dynasty [about 1.450-1.290 BC], of unknown origin. Inscription: "Delta wine for the Osiris Nedkhmet".

Sample BM3: Pink jar, numbered EA 51187. From Early Dynastic period [2.950-2.575 BC], found at the grave 5 of cemetery 3 in Faras, Nubia. Without inscription.

Sample CM1: Wine jar, numbered JE 62313. From 18th Dynasty, Tutankhamun's reign [1.332-1.322 BC], found at the tomb of Tutankhamun [KV 62] in Western Thebes. Inscription: "Year 5. Wine of the Estate of Tutankhamun, Ruler of the Southern On, l.p.h., [in] the Western River. Chief vintner Khaa".

Sample CM2: Wine jar, numbered JE 57356. From 18th Dynasty [1.539-1.292 BC], found at el-Amarna. Without inscription.

EA=*Egyptian Archaeology* number of the British Museum in London.
JE=*Journal d'Entrée* number of the Egyptian Museum in Cairo.

Table 1: Archaeological samples collected from ancient Egyptian pottery jars.

analysis, by special permissions of the Egyptian Supreme Council for Antiquities [SCA] and the Egyptian Museum in Cairo (Egypt) as well as the British Museum in London (UK). The residues were collected from three Egyptian pottery jars at the British Museum, which are named BM samples here, and two pottery jars at the Egyptian Museum in Cairo, named CM samples. A short description of the objects, dating periods and sites, if known, is included in Table 1.

Sample CM1 was a dry deposit of dark brown color from the bottom of a wine-jar; samples BM1 and CM2 were thin encrustations on the inside of pottery jars; samples BM2 and BM3 were obtained by scraping the inside surface of the jar, not having visible deposits. Alkaline fusion was only performed on the CM1 sample because it is a deposit residue of dark-brown color. Due to the nature of the other samples, alkaline fusion was not possible.

A blank as a sample control was also included in this study to identify possible interference in ceramics not due to tartaric acid. It was a pottery handle of ancient Egyptian origin not having come into contact with vessel contents.

Standards and reagents

Standard of L-tartaric acid [99% purity] was purchased from Aldrich Chemical Co [Steinheim, Germany] and prepared at a concentration of 100 mg/L in water. Standard of syringic acid [98%] from Fluka Chemie AG [Buchs, Switzerland] was prepared at a concentration of 100 mg/L in methanol-water [20:80, v/v]. The working solution of 100 μg/L was made diluting the standard solutions with the LC mobile phase [0.1% formic

acid in water/acetonitrile, 90:10]. Acetonitrile and methanol of HPLC grade were purchased from SDS [Peypin, France], formic acid and ethyl acetate [99%] from Panreac [Barcelona, Spain], potassium hydroxide pellets [85%] from Carlo Erba (Milano, Italy) and ultrapure water [Milli-Q] was obtained from Millipore System [Bedford, MA, USA].

Sample preparation

An amount of ~ 2 mg of pulverized residue was extracted with 5 mL of 0.1% of formic acid in water/methanol [80:20, v/v] with magnetic stirring and ultrasound. The liquid was centrifuged for 15 min at 1620 g, the supernatant was concentrated under nitrogen to one-fifth volume for CM samples and 0.1 volume for BM samples and, finally, they were filtered with an acrodisc 13 CR PTFE 0.45μm [Waters, Massachusetts, USA]. Alkaline fusion was performed by addition of potassium hidroxide pellets [~ 0.2 g] to the sample described above under heating for 5 min, acidification and finally extraction with ethyl acetate, following the previously published literature (Singleton, 1996; Zugla and Kiss, 1987).

Instrumentation

Analyses were carried out using a liquid chromatograph with a mass spectrometer in tandem mode. LC equipment was an Agilent 1100 [Waldbronn, Germany] with a quaternary pump. A Waters Atlantis C_{18} column [2.1 x 150 mm i.d., 5μm] was used at ambient temperature and the injected volume was 15μL. A constant flow rate of 200 μL/min was used with two elution solvents: 0.1% formic acid in water, solvent A, and

LC/MS/MS Optimum conditions		
MS/MS ions	(*m/z* (rel. abundance, %))	
Tartaric acid: Mw= 150	149 (100), 87 (22)	DP (V)=-25; CE (V)=-20
Syringic acid: Mw= 198	197 (100), 182 (28)	DP (V)=-30; CE (V)=-20

Table 2: LC/MS/MS optimum conditions for tartaric acid and syringic acid MS/MS detection in the negative mode.

acetonitrile, solvent B. The gradient was initially isocratic until minute 5 with 100% of solvent A; at minute 10 solvents were A/B [80:20] and a second isocratic step was performed from minute 15 to 30 with solvents A/B [50:50]. The mass spectrometer was an API 3000 triple quadrupole MS/MS System [PE Sciex, Concord, ON, Canada], equipped with a Turbo ion spray source operating in negative-ion mode for monitoring ions of deprotonated molecules [M-H]⁻.

Method optimization

Method selectivity was based on the requirement to find a column with a better retention of polar compounds, in a water mobile phase, than normally achieved by a conventional C_{18} column. Preliminary studies, data not shown, led us to select an Atlantis [Waters] column. Ammonium formiate and formic acid/water mobile phases were tested for peak shape optimization, maximum of retention, and ionization of the compounds. MS/MS conditions were optimized for tartaric and syringic acids: capillary voltage – 4500V, curtain gas is N_2 at 12 [arbitrary units], nebulizer gas is N_2 at 10 [arbitrary units], collision gas is N_2 at 4 [arbitrary units], focusing potential – 200V, entrance potential is N_2 at 10V, collision cell exit potential –15V, drying gas is N_2 heated to 400ºC and introduced at a flow rate of 6500 cm³/min. Declustering potential [DP] and collision energy [CE] were optimized, as it is shown in Table 2, in infusions of individual standard solutions of 1 mg/L at a constant flow-rate of 5µL/min into the mass spectrometer using a syringe pump model 11 [Harvard Apparatus, Holliston, MA, USA]. The DP was varied from 0 to 200V and the CE from –5 to –45V, which were optimized for maximum sensitivity of the multiple reaction monitoring [MRM] signal.

In order to choose fragmentation patterns of m/z (Q1)→ m/z (Q3) ions for the MRM transitions, product ion scan mass spectra were produced by collision-activated dissociation [CAD] of selected precursor ions in the collision cell of the triple quadrupole mass spectrometer, and analyzed using the second analyzer of the instrument. Full-scan data acquisition was performed scanning from *m/z* 80 to 800 in profile mode, using a scan time of 2s with a step size of 0.1u and a pause

between each scan of 2ms. In order to enhance sensitivity, shorter ranges were scanned from 100 to 250 u for tartaric acid. Confirmation of the presence of tartaric acid was also done, when it was possible, by injection of samples in product ion scan of 149, scanning from 70 to 160 u using a scan time of 2s. When low concentrations are present, the injections in single ion monitoring [SIM] mode or multiple reaction monitoring [MRM] mode were performed.

The spectra generated for tartaric acid with a mass wheight [M_w] of 150 using full-scan in the negative ion mode showed the deprotonated molecule [M – H]⁻ with an optimum CE of -25V. The product ion scan of *m/z* 149 gives *m/z* 87, due to a loss of the COOH and OH groups. In this manner, the MRM method is established between ions 149 and 87 at a CE of -20V. The spectra generated for syringic acid [M_w 198] in the negative ion mode showed the deprotonated molecule [M – H]⁻ with an optimum DP of -30V. The product ion scan observed for syringic acid [*m/z* 197] gave a loss of the CH_3 group, providing the [M – H – CH_3]⁻ • anion radical at *m/z* 182. In this manner, the MRM method was established between ions 197 and 182 at a CE of -20V.

Limit Ordinary of Detection in MRM mode was calculated by repeated injections [n=10] of the working solution of 15 µL injected, at a signal-to-noise ratio [S/N] of 3 and the value obtained was 0.05 µg/L for both compounds.

RESULTS AND DISCUSSION

Identification of tartaric acid

The presence of tartaric acid in the archaeological residues was first investigated in the deposit residue of CM1 sample. Injection of this sample in full scan mode produced a peak in the *m/z* 149 trace at a retention time of 2.64 min, as shown in Figure B. The product ion scan of 149, scanning from 80 to 152 u, gave the mass spectra of 87 in the CM1 sample and in the standard of tartaric acid.

This sample was also injected in SIM mode of *m/z* 149, see Figure C, and also in MRM of the transition *m/z* 149 → 87, see Figure D, thus giving a peak in the chromatograms at the same

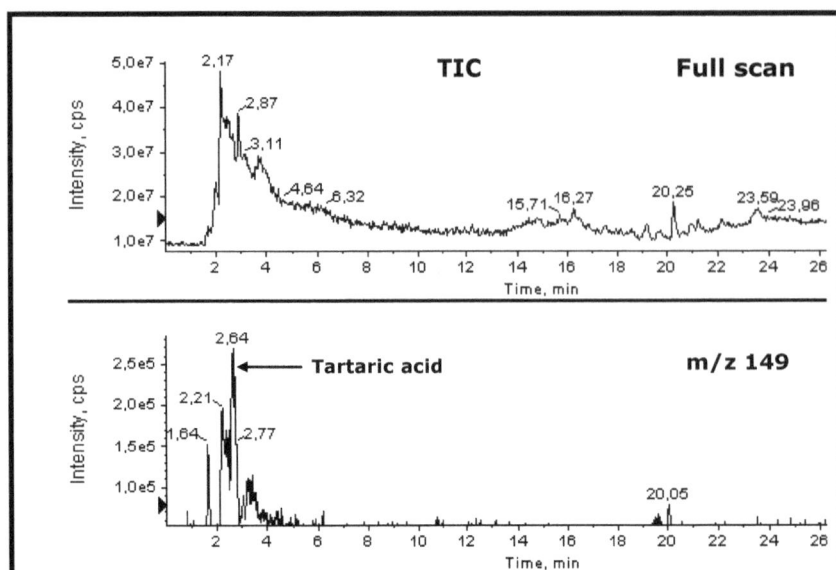

Figure B: Total ion chromatogram [TIC] in full-scan mode for tartaric acid in CM1 sample scanning from 100 to 250 u.

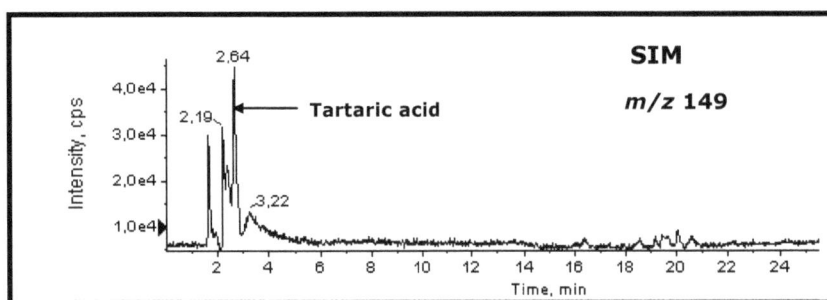

Figure C: LC/MS/MS chromatogram in SIM mode for tartaric acid in CM1 sample.

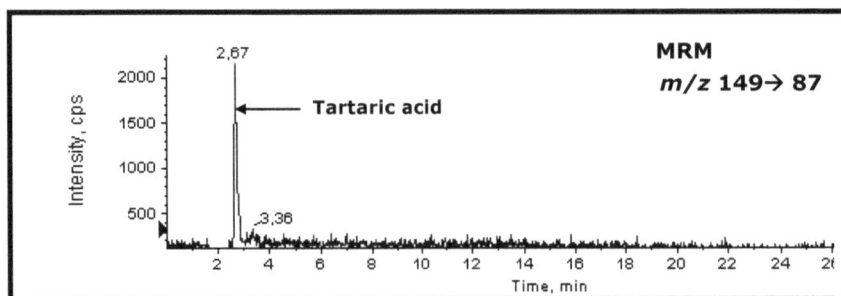

Figure D: LC/MS/MS chromatogram in MRM mode using m/z 149→87 transition for tartaric acid in CM1 sample.

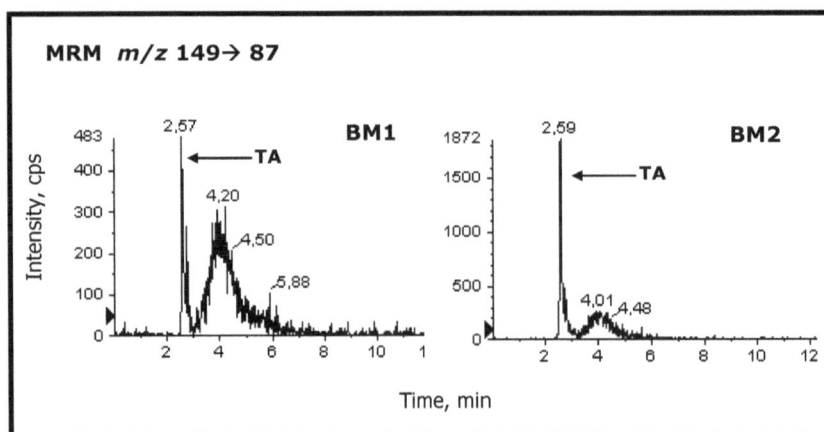

Figure E: LC/MS/MS chromatogram in MRM mode using m/z 149→87 transition for tartaric acid (TA) peak in BM1 and BM2 samples.

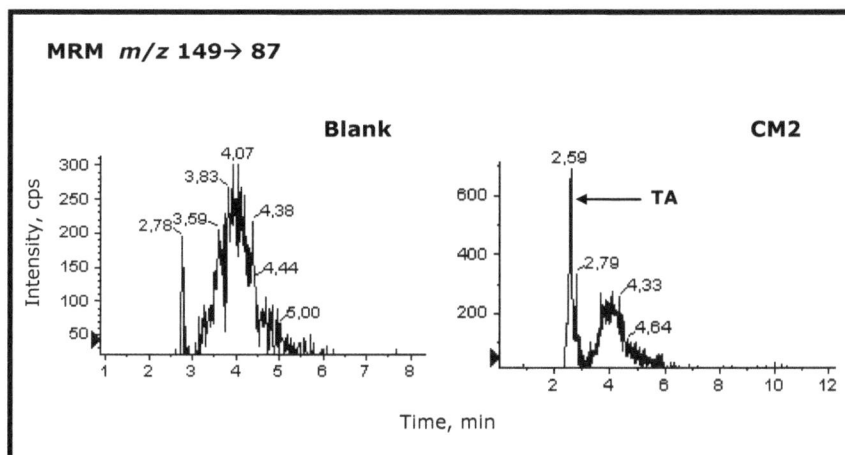

Figure F: LC/MS/MS chromatogram in MRM mode using m/z 149→87 transition for tartaric acid (TA) peak in CM2 sample and the blank. No tartaric acid is present in the blank.

retention time of the standard injected in the same conditions.

All the other samples, obtained from jar incrustations and scrapings, were also analyzed in full-scan mode but, unfortunately, there was no result for tartaric acid, probably due to the low concentration present in these kinds of samples. As the lowest detection limits using LC/MS/MS can be achieved in MRM mode, this was the method of choice for the rest of samples.

Figure E and Figure F show the MS/MS chromatograms corresponding to samples BM1, BM2 and CM2 where tartaric acid was positively identified, as well as the chromatogram of the pottery blank which was scraped from an ancient Egyptian pottery handle.

Due to the fact that the MRM chromatogram of the blank shows a peak at a retention time close to that of tartaric acid, the positive identification was done on the basis of the retention time compared with tartaric acid standard and by spiking the sample with tartaric solution.

The chromatogram in MRM mode corresponding to the BM3 sample [Figure G] showed no peak at the retention time of tartaric standard but a peak at 2.76 min, the same as in the blank [see Figure F]. The sample BM3 was spiked with tartaric acid standard which demonstrated that no tartaric acid was present, as shows Figure H. The retention time of the spiked tartaric acid at 2.55 min did not correspond with the unknown peak at 2.76 min.

In view of the fact that analysis of the pottery blank also showed this peak at 2.78 min, see Figure F, and this led us to the conclusion that it was due to the ceramic. Note that a peak at 2.79 min is also present in the CM2 sample, see Figure F, which was a jar incrustation.

The positive results for tartaric acid obtained in samples BM1, BM2, CM1 and CM2 from Egyptian jars confirm they were used as wine containers, being wine-jars of type (see LÄ VI, 1986).

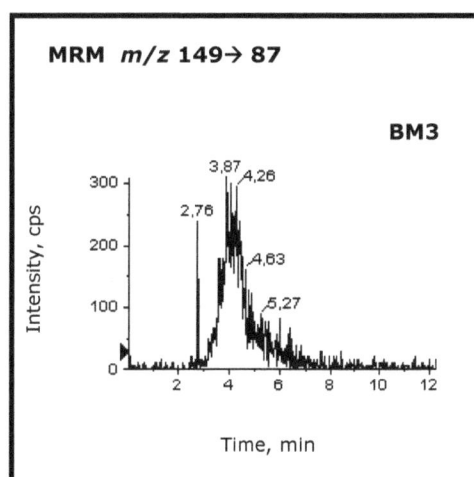

Figure G: LC/MS/MS chromatogram in MRM mode using m/z 149→87 transition for tartaric acid in BM3 sample.

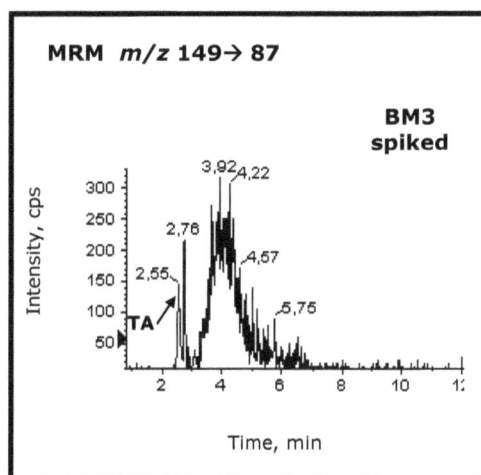

Figure H: LC/MS/MS chromatogram in MRM mode using m/z 149→87 transition for tartaric acid (TA) in BM3 sample spiked with standard of tartaric acid.

49

CM1 sample before alkaline fusion

MRM
m/z 197→ 182

No syringic acid is present

(chromatogram: Intensity, cps vs. Time, min; peaks labelled 18,25 19,08 21,49)

CM1 sample after alkaline fusion

MRM
m/z 197→ 182

Syringic acid

(chromatogram: Intensity, cps vs. Time, min; inset peaks labelled 18,25 18,61 19,08; main peaks labelled 21,49 18,25 18,61 21,72)

Syringic acid standard

MRM
m/z 197→ 182

(chromatogram: Intensity, cps vs. Time, min; peak labelled 18,61)

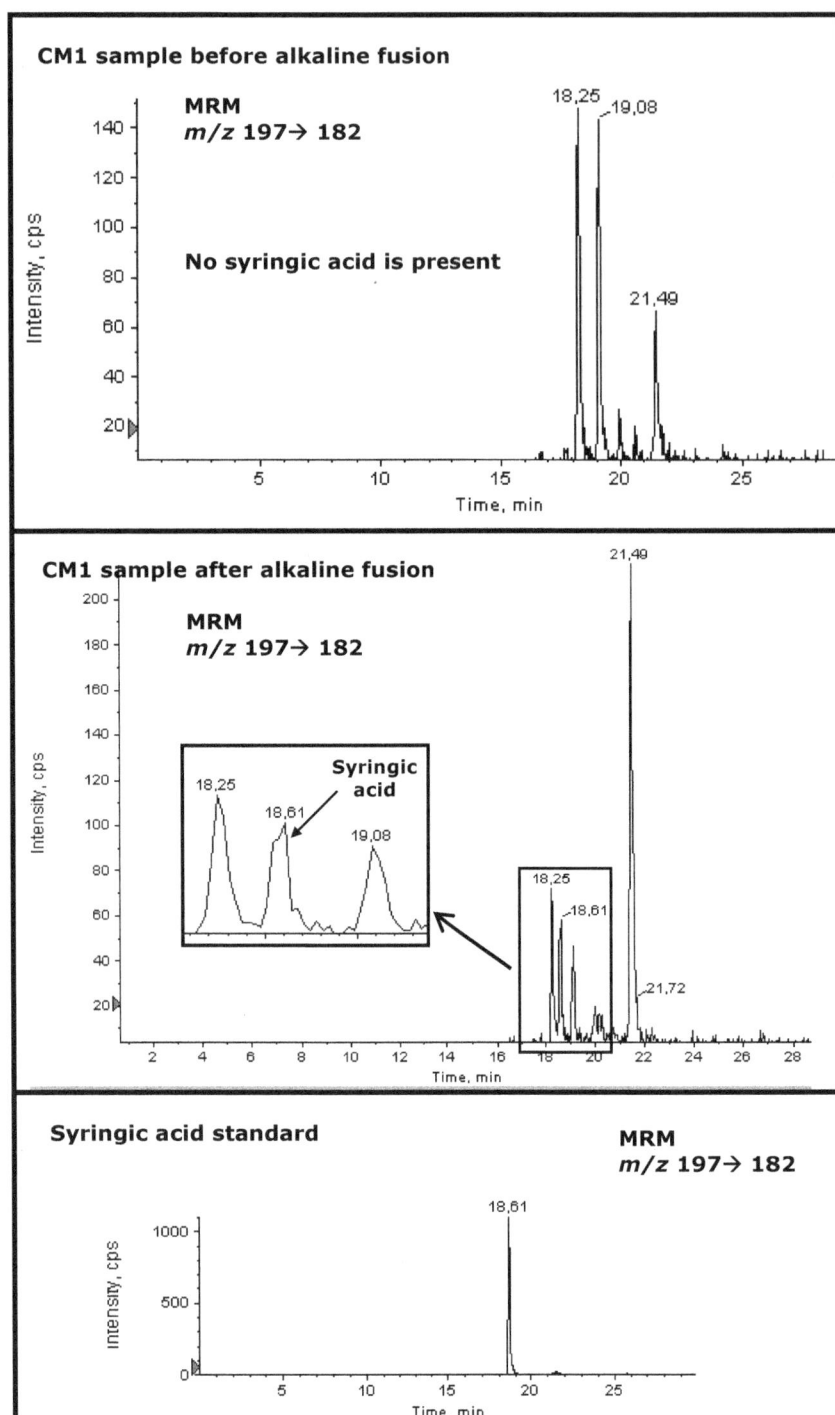

Figure I: LC/MS/MS chromatograms in MRM mode using m/z 197→182 transition for syringic acid in CM1 sample before and after the alkaline oxidation, and for the standard of syringic acid. Syringic acid is present after the alkaline reaction of the CM1 sample.

Tartaric absence does not necessarily mean a container was not used for wine, according to Singleton (1996). However, the jar from which the BM3 sample was collected does not correspond to a wine-jar type (see LÄ VI, 1986).

Identification of syringic acid

In order to study the color of ancient Egyptian wines, we focussed on determining the presence of malvidin, because no other juice or liquid from the ancient wine areas of Near East and Mediterranean region is high in malvidin apart from those coming from red grapes (Singleton, 1996). Malvidin-3-glucoside is the major anthocyanin that gives the red color to young red wines. Aging of wine changes the red-purple color of wine into a more red-brown hue, which has been attributed to the formation of anthocyanin-derived pigments. These pigments are more stable due to chemical reactions involving malvidin and phenolic compounds (Mateus *et al*, 2002; Remy,

2000) or involving non phenolic compounds (Atanasova *et al*, 2002; Fulcrand *et al*, 1998) which are present in wines. However, the stability and evolution of wine pigments over thousands of years are still unknown. Polymerized pigments isolation and identification in aged wines was reported to be difficult, especially because their levels are much lower than those of original anthocyanins (Para and Riviere, 1982), and because malvidin is a basic structural component of wine pigments (Mateus *et al*, 2002).

Alkaline fusion was carried out with the CM1 sample, which was a dark brown deposit found inside a wine-jar. This wine-jar [JE 62313 in the Cairo Museum] was found in 1922 at king Tutankhamun's tomb by Howard Carter. By alkaline fusion of the sample of residue, and according to the reaction described by Zugla and Kiss (1987) for chromonoid compounds, malvidin in the structure of the polymerized pigment would react, as shown in Figure A [see chapter III.2.2.], breaking the C ring in two steps and releasing syringic acid.

The sample of CM1 was analyzed before the alkaline fusion and after it, see Figure I, by LC/MS/MS using the MRM acquisition mode, as the previous full scan gave no signal for the *m/z* 197 ion.

The MS/MS chromatogram at *m/z* 197 → *m/z* 182 ions of the fragmentation pattern after the alkaline fusion showed a peak of syringic acid at 18.61 min, as can be seen in Figure I. The retention time was confirmed by comparison with that of the standard of syringic acid which had a peak at min 18.61, as shows Figure I.

On the contrary, before the alkaline fusion of CM1 sample there was no peak at the retention time of the standard. These results confirm that syringic acid obtained after oxidation of the sample came from polymerized malvidin, having a red grape origin. Due to this new data we can now add to the inscription of this wine jar [see Table 1] a new information about the kind of wine which contained. In this case, a red wine.

Conclusion

Presented is a new LC/MS/MS method for the identification of tartaric acid and syringic acid using a triple quadrupole mass spectrometer. This method proposed is particularly suitable in terms of selectivity and sensitivity for archaeological pottery analysis of tartaric acid, whether there are visible residues or not. Moreover, the new method has allowed for the first time to identify not only the presence of wine, but also to reveal the red grape origin of the wine contained in a jar belonging to the tomb of king Tutankhamun, through LC/MS/MS detection of syringic acid from polymerized malvidin. Here we have the key to uncover the origins of oenology, as well as opening future investigations into the color of ancient wines.

III.5.2. THE ORIGIN OF THE ANCIENT EGYPTIAN DRINK *SHEDEH* REVEALED USING LC/MS/MS

"Reprinted from Journal of the Archaeological Science 33 (2006), Guasch-Jané MR., Andrés-Lacueva C., Jáuregui O. and Lamuela-Raventós RM., "The Origin of the Ancient Egyptian drink Shedeh revealed using LC/MS/MS", p. 98-101. Copyright [2008], with permission from Elsevier".

Ancient Egyptians were buried with the most precious food and drink as sustenance for their afterlife. One of these was *Shedeh*, the most valued and appreciated beverage in ancient Egypt. The botanic origin of *Shedeh* remains unclear as no mention of its raw material has survived.

Some scholars have proposed that *Shedeh* was a pomegranate wine, while others, a grape wine. Presented here is the first ever analytical evidence of *Shedeh*'s origin, through the analysis of a sample of a residue from an extraordinarily well preserved *Shedeh* amphora from king Tutankhamun's tomb. The previously developed LC/MS/MS wine markers method for archaeological samples is used, the results revealing *Shedeh* has a red grape origin.

Introduction

An ancient Egyptian text described the *Shedeh* drink as a gift from the sun god Ra to his sons (Derchain, 1965), bestowing it with divine power, ensuring it was of the highest quality, and that *Shedeh* was served in the most valuable vases. However, the real meaning of the name of this Egyptian drink, *Shedeh*, which appeared at the end of the 18th Dynasty [about 1.350 BC], is unknown. The two main references on Egyptian lexis and culture do not agree on a definition: "*Shedeh* could be pomegranate wine" (Helck, 1977) or "a beverage akin to wine" (Erman and Grapow, 1930).

A study of *Shedeh* inscriptions on pottery jars concluded that it could be more closely identified with a traditional wine and, specifically, a cooked wine was proposed (Tallet, 1995). However, to date, the botanical origin of *Shedeh* has never been proven.

To discover the true origin of this Egyptian beverage, the previously developed wine markers method (Guasch-Jané *et al*, 2004) using liquid chromatography coupled to mass spectrometry in tandem mode [LC/MS/MS], was applied in the first ever scientific research on the raw material of *Shedeh*. Two wine markers in archaeology, tartaric acid, and syringic acid derived from malvidin-3-glucoside, were investigated for in a residue from an extraordinary *Shedeh* amphora.

Shedeh's significance

The name *Shedeh* appeared inscribed on the labels of Egyptian two-handled pottery amphorae at the site of el-Amarna, belonging to the reign of Akhenaten, late 18th Dynasty. Its name showed it was a beverage different from the traditional (grape-)wine, whose Egyptian name was *Irp* (Erman and Grapow, 1926). An example of the importance of *Shedeh* in ancient Egyptian times was the fact that it was cited in the Egyptian romantic poetry, where *Shedeh* was associated with a lover's voice (Tallet, 1995). During the Ramessid [1.292-1.075 BC] and Ptolemaic [305-30 BC] periods, the *Shedeh* drink was recorded on temple inscriptions, and used as a religious offering as well as for embalming (Tallet, 1995).

Hundreds of inscriptions on amphorae dated late 18th-19th Dynasty from Malkata, el-Amarna, the Ramesseum and Deir el-Medina have been found, most of them being shards now. According to Tallet (1995), it is significant that only fifteen of them have been documented bearing the name *Shedeh*, from el-Amarna, Tutankhamun's tomb at Western Thebes and Maya's tomb at Saqqara. *Shedeh* inscriptions included the year, quality, estate, region, and vintner's name as with the best wines of that age.

One *Shedeh* inscription on a complete amphora [see Figure 6.2] was found in 1922 by Howard Carter at the intact Burial chamber of Tutankhamun [1.333-1.323 BC]. On finding the amphora, Carter wrote on the archaeological card: "What exactly *Shedeh* is, is not known. A kind of beer, date-wine etc are possible" (Carter, 2000-2003).

Some authors have translated the word *Shedeh* as pomegranate wine (Hope, 1993). This, however, is considered a tenuous proposal by Tallet (1995) due to the fact that it is based on a supposition. This supposition was established by Loret (1892) from a text from the reign of Ramses II [1.279-1.213 BC], the papyrus Anastasi IV [6-7], which referred to a garden in which two fruits were found: grapes and pomegranates. The three drinks obtained from them were wine, must and *Shedeh*. Loret suggested that *Shedeh* was a pomegranate-wine (1892). Since then, Derchain (1965) and Tallet (1995) have proposed *Shedeh* could have been a grape-wine with a distinct and more elaborate preparation. Despite the substantial information regarding all aspects of life in ancient Egypt recorded on temples, tomb walls and papyrus, the botanical origin of *Shedeh* has never been revealed to us in the ancient Egyptian texts. The only known report on the preparation of *Shedeh* was described on the Papyrus Salt 825 from Late period [715-332 BC]. However, this text lacks information on the raw material: "It is [...] repeat the filtration; heating again. This is the way to prepare the *Shedeh*" (Derchain, 1965), see

Figure 6.1. Due to a gap in this papyrus, the initial ingredient is not known. Moreover, the only information we have on the preparation of *Shedeh* is on an inscription at the temple of Dendera [MD 4,77a] as "the beautiful work of Horus in the laboratory through the cooked extracts of Shesmu, the God of the press" (Derchain, 1965). Derchain (1965) concluded that even if *Shedeh* was a type of wine, the description on the Papyrus Salt 825 eliminates the possibility that it could be must or ordinary wine because they are not heated.

The sample

With permission of the Egyptian Supreme Council for Antiquities and the Egyptian Museum in Cairo, a sample of the dry black residue from inside Tutankhamun's *Shedeh* amphora, *Journal d'Entrée* number 62315 [see Figure 6.2] from the Egyptian Museum, was taken for analysis.

In 1922 Carter found this well preserved amphora lying on the ground beside the south wall, inside the Burial chamber of king Tutankhamun's tomb, in the Valley of Kings [KV 62] at Western Thebes, Egypt. Food and wine were placed on the Annexe chamber of Tutankhamun's tomb, however, three amphorae were found inside the Burial chamber, placed beside the south, west, and east walls respectively. The two amphorae at the west and east positions were labelled *Irp* (Holthoer, 1993).

The hieratic inscription on the amphora JE 62315 records: "Year 5. *Shedeh* of very good quality of the Estate of Aten of the Western River. Chief vintner *Rer*" and "very good" is also stipulated on the top of the amphora (Černy, 1965).

206

Amphora JE 62315, Egyptian Museum in Cairo.
Copyright: Griffith Institute, Oxford.

Results and discussion

The previously developed LC/MS/MS method for the identification of wine markers in archaeological samples (Guasch-Jané *et al*, 2004) was employed, as follows. In brief, an amount of approximately ~2mg of sample was extracted with water:methanol [80:20, v:v] containing 0.1% formic acid. An alkaline fusion was performed with potassium hydroxide pellets in the same quantity as well. The extracts were injected in the LC/MS/MS system in multiple reaction monitoring [MRM] mode, as the most sensitive MS method, which allows compound confirmation, through a parent and a product ion, to be compared with the standard.

Tartaric acid, the grape marker in archaeology (Michel *et al*, 1993) exclusively found in grapes in the Mediterranean and Near East areas, was first investigated in the sample. On the MRM chromatogram at m/z 149→87 transition for tartaric acid [M_w 150], a peak at retention time of 2.61 min. appeared at the same retention time of the tartaric acid standard injected in the same conditions, see Figure J, showing the presence of tartaric acid in the *Shedeh* sample.

Moreover, the presence of syringic acid, recently confirmed as a red wine marker for archaeological samples (Guasch-Jané *et al*, 2004), was also investigated in the sample, before and after performing alkaline oxidation.

Identification of syringic acid was done by injection of the sample in MRM mode of the m/z 197→182 transition. Before alkaline fusion, no peak of syringic acid [M_w 198] was detected in the MRM chromatogram [see Figure K] at 18.35 min. of retention time for syringic acid standard. However, after performing this alkaline fusion, a peak of syringic acid at 18.35 min. was identified in the sample, see Figure K, released from the main red wine pigment malvidin-3-glucoside through the breaking down of the polymerized pigment which had been formed over time (Mateus *et al*, 2002).

Conclusion

By applying the previously developed LC/MS/MS wine markers method to a residue sample from Tutankhamun's *Shedeh* amphora num. JE 62315 at the Egyptian Museum in Cairo, tartaric acid and syringic acid which are the markers for *Vitis vinifera* and the red cultivars respectively, were identified. The results allow to reveal for the first time that the *Shedeh* residue sample came from grapes, in particular red grapes.

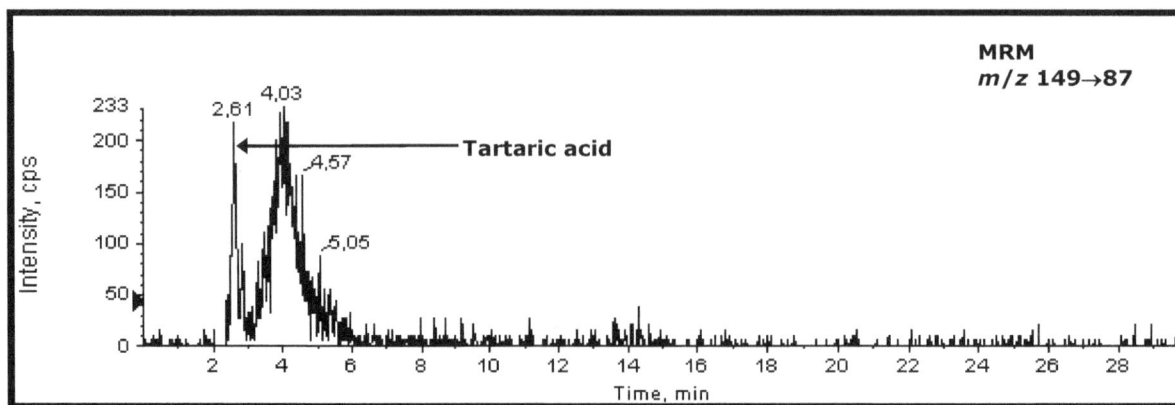

Figure J: LC/MS/MS chromatogram in MRM mode using m/z 149→87 transition for tartaric acid is identified in the sample from the *Shedeh* amphora.

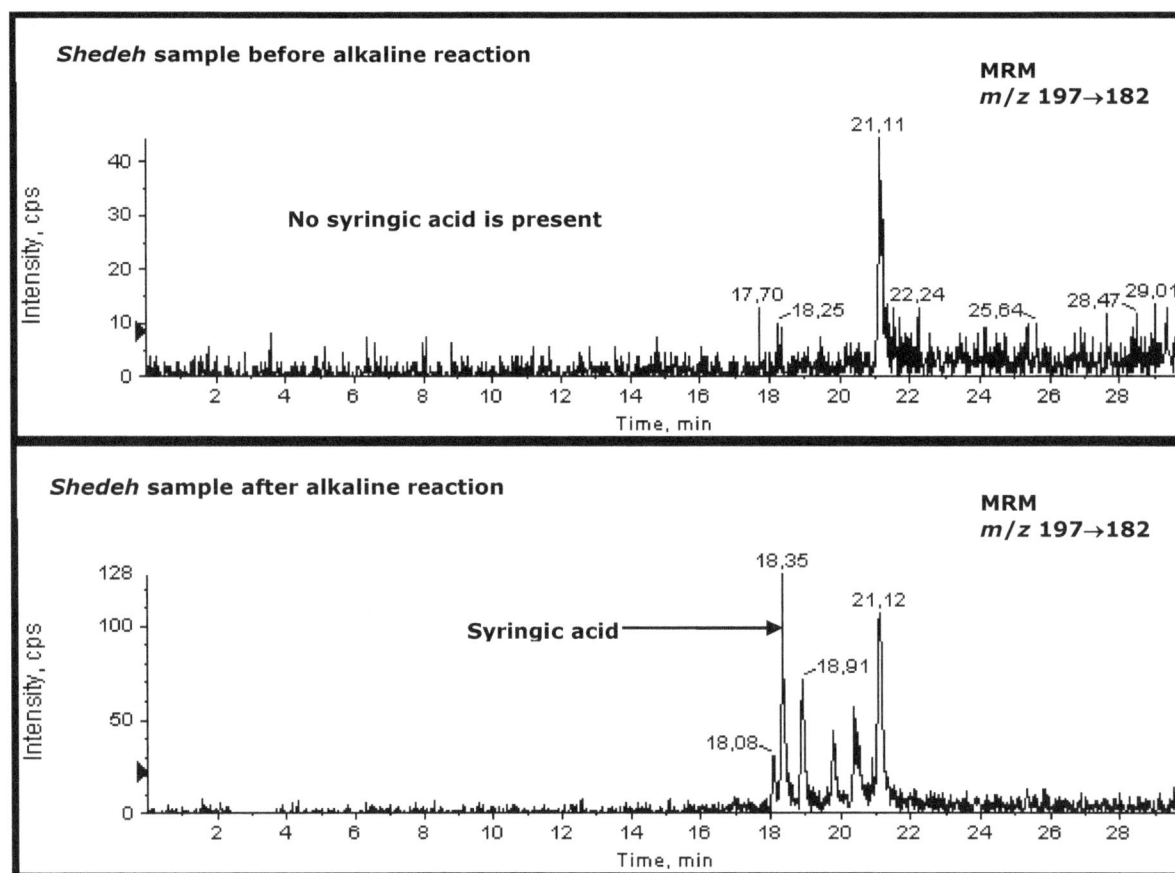

Figure K: LC/MS/MS chromatogram in MRM mode using m/z 197→182 for syringic acid, before and after the alkaline reaction, in the sample from the *Shedeh* amphora. The red grape marker syringic acid is not present in the sample before the alkaline oxidation, as it is in a more complex form. By performing the alkaline reaction to the sample, a peak of syringic acid is identified having been released from malvidin-3-glucoside in the pigment.

III.5.3. FIRST EVIDENCE OF WHITE WINE IN ANCIENT EGYPT FROM TUTANKHAMUN'S TOMB

Wine has been considered to have been mainly red in ancient Egypt linked with the blood of Osiris, the God of resurrection. No text that refers to white wines from the Dynastic period [3.150-332 BC] exists. The first white wine from ancient Egypt was made near Alexandria during the third century. To investigate for the presence of white wine in ancient Egypt, dry residue samples from King Tutankhamun's amphorae displayed on the Egyptian Museum in Cairo are studied in this article using the LC/MS/MS method for wine markers. This investigation into the existence of white wines in Tutankhamun's tomb allows us to shed new light on the symbolism of white wine in ancient Egypt.

Introduction

In ancient Egypt, the royal family and the upper classes drank wine, which was also thought to be suitable among the necessities for a good afterlife (James, 1996). Viticulture and wine-making scenes were represented on walls of private tombs from the Old Kingdom period [2.575-2.150 BC] and, lately, during the New Kingdom [1.539-1.075 BC] wine jars included the year of harvest, the ownership, the quality and the name of the wine-maker as well (James, 1996).

Wine offerings to gods performed by the Pharaoh were often shown on the walls of Egyptian temples, recording details of festivals like the Heb-Sed and the New Year's celebration of the flooding of the Nile, as well as coronation ceremonies (Poo, 1995). Wine had religious significance in offering liturgies, it was offered to the dead for their afterlife, and wine is among the funerary offerings stated in the Pyramid Texts, being the main drink after the king's ascension to heaven (Poo, 1995).

The color of wine was not referred to on the walls of tombs, temples or on New Kingdom inscribed jars. According to Lucas (1962), no literary reference to the color of grapes grown in ancient Egypt can be traced. The grapes on the vines painted on walls of the Egyptian tombs were mainly painted in a dark color. However, they have been considered to range from light green to blackish blue, while the color of the extracted juice varies from a light pink to a dark red which could be related to local conventions or attributed to artistic whim (Poo, 1995). Red wine symbolized the rebirth of the dead, being compared with the blood of God Osiris, the first who resurrected

(Cherpion, 1999).

The study of archaeological samples from wine amphorae, first based on the identification of the presence of tartaric acid as a grape wine marker, nowadays can also be focused on the color of the wine through the identification of syringic acid as a red wine marker (Guasch-Jané *et al*, 2004). Syringic acid is released from the main red grape pigment, malvidin-3-glucoside, through the breaking down of the complex molecule formed over time (Mateus *et al*, 2002). The only two amphorae previously studied from Tutankhamun's collection (Guasch-Jané *et al*, 2004 and 2006A) have been shown to contain red wine. One was an amphora [numbered *Journal d'Entrée* 62313 at the Egyptian Museum in Cairo] the inscription indicating it contained *Irp* [wine], while the other amphora [numbered JE 62315] contained *Shedeh*. Both tartaric and syringic acids were identified in the samples from these two amphorae (Guasch-Jané *et al*, 2004; 2006A). The artistic and textual records suggest that red wine predominated during Pharaonic Egypt (Murray, 2000).

White wine in ancient Egypt

It has been a matter of speculation as to whether white wine was ever made in Dynastic Egypt (Murray, 2000). Originally mentioned in the Pyramid Texts, the *Irp* (wine) *abesh* cited in a text found in the tomb of Ukh-Hotep at Meir was suggested as the first evidence of white wine (Blackman, 1915), however, it is now considered to have been a type of wine container (Murray, 2000). The oldest textual evidence of white wines in ancient Egypt dates to the third century AD, when the Greek Athenaeus [170-230 AD] from Naukratis, Egypt, described in the book "Sophists at Dinner" the wine from Mariut as being: "...excellent, white, pleasant, fragrant, easily assimilated, thin, not likely to go to the head, and diuretic". The wine from Mariut, located in the southwest of Alexandria, was regarded to have been one of the best wines at that time (Lesko, 1996). Earlier, during the first century BC the Latin poet Virgil spoke in praise of the white grapes from Mariut (Berget, 1934; Virgil, 1586).

Tutankhamun's amphorae

Twenty-six two-handled amphorae were placed for the burial of King Tutankhamun [1.332-1.322 BC] in his tomb at the Valley of Kings [KV 62] in Western Thebes (Holthoer, 1993). When the archaeologist Howard Carter found them in 1922, some of the amphorae were just fragments of the top of the jars, a few of them were intact sealed amphorae while others had the mud seal broken (Holthoer, 1993). The amphorae were mainly located in the small Annexe chamber in no particular order. However, three of them were found inside the Burial chamber (Carter, 1927). The inscriptions on Tutankhamun's amphorae show the name of the product, the year, the property and the place of origin, and the name of the vintner in chief but not the color of these wines.

From the 26 amphorae of Tutankhamun's tomb, twelve amphorae were found intact by Carter but with the mud seal broken or without the entire cap. So that no further damage would be done to the intact sealed amphorae now at the Egyptian Museum in Cairo [see Figure 5.2.] these twelve amphorae were examined and dry residues were found inside 6 of them. With the permission of the Egyptian Supreme Council of Antiquities and the Egyptian Museum, a small quantity of sample from each one of these six amphorae was collected for analysis.

With the aim of verifying whether the remaining amphorae contained red or white wines, samples of residues from six of the amphorae of Tutankhamun's collection at the Egyptian Museum in Cairo [Figure 5.2.] are studied by applying the previously published LC/MS/MS wine markers method (Guasch-Jané *et al*, 2004) for archaeological samples.

Wines in Tutankhamun's Burial chamber

Three amphorae were found at the Burial chamber of Tutankhamun, which contained the sarcophagus. They were lying on the ground between the wall and the shrine placed on the west [*Journal d'Entrée* 62314], east [JE 62316] and south [JE 62315] walls. They were lacking their mud seals. The inscriptions indicate that two of the amphorae [JE 62314 and JE 62316] contained *Irp*, being traditional grape-wine. Nevertheless, the amphora at the south wall [JE 62315] contained very good *Shedeh*, a highly appreciated red grape-wine with a more elaborate preparation (Tallet, 1995; Guasch-Jané *et al*, 2004).

Ancient Egyptians believed the universe was not set in order until the dead king had been buried with proper rites to allow him to embark successfully on his eternal life (Taylor, 2001). For this reason, Egyptian Pharaohs were buried at special sacred places such as the Valley of Kings in Western Thebes. During the New Kingdom period [1.543-1.078 BC], the gods Ra and Osiris were considered to give rebirth to the dead. The royal tombs internal features reproduce the underworld, the tomb being a cosmogram (Taylor, 2001). Tutankhamun's Burial chamber had an east-west orientation in which the wall decoration scenes are being orientated towards the west (Reeves, 1990). One amphora labeled *Irp* was placed beside the east wall, where the picture shows the mummified king. Another *Irp* amphora was placed to the west. The scenes there are extracted from the Amduat, the book of "What is in the Underworld." The twelve baboon deities shown represent the twelve hours of the night through which the sun, and the king, must travel to their rebirth at dawn (Reeves,

1990).

The Samples

Following the *Journal d'Entrée* numbers of the Egyptian Museum [EM], the samples from the six amphorae are listed down here. The translation into English of the hieratic inscriptions of these amphorae by Černý (1965) is included (see also Beinlich and Saleh, 1989), and the location of the amphorae inside the tomb of Tutankhamun, as well as the color of the samples of residues.

The samples are:

EM1: Amphora no. JE 62301; Inscription: "Year 5. Wine of the Estate of Aten of the Western River. Chief vintner Pinehas"; Found at the Annexe lying on the floor beside the west wall; The color of the residue is yellowish.

EM2: Amphora no. JE 62302; Inscription: "Vizier Pentu", and charcoal mark on one side; Found at the Annexe lying on the floor towards the north; Yellowish color residue.

EM3: Amphora no. JE 62303; Inscription: "Year 4. Wine of the Estate of Aten, may he live, be prosperous and healthy, of the Western River. Chief vintner Nen"; Found at the Annexe lying on the floor along the east wall; Pale brown color residue.

EM4: Amphora no. JE 62312; Inscription: "Year 5. Sweet wine of the Estate of Aten of the Western River. Chief vintner Nakht", and charcoal mark below the inscription; Found at the Annexe lying on the floor; Yellowish color residue.

EM5: Amphora no. JE 62314; Inscription: "Year 9. Wine of the Estate of Aten of the Western River. Chief vintner Sennufe", and stamp on handle: "Estate of Aten"; Found at the Burial Chamber beside the west wall; Dark-blackish color residue.

EM6: Amphora no. JE 62316; Inscription: "Year 5. Wine of the Estate of Tutankhamun, Ruler of the Southern On, in the Western River. Chief vintner Khaa", and stamp on handle: "Ruler's Estate"; Found at the Burial Chamber beside the east wall; Pale brown color residue.

Results

The previously developed method for the identification of wine markers in archaeology (Guasch-Jané *et al*, 2004), using liquid chromatography coupled to mass spectrometry in tandem mode [LC/MS/MS] technique, was applied to the analysis of the samples. An amount of approximately ~2 mg of each one of the samples was extracted with water:methanol containing 0.1% formic acid [80:20, v:v]. Alkaline fusion (Guasch-Jané *et al*, 2004) was performed with

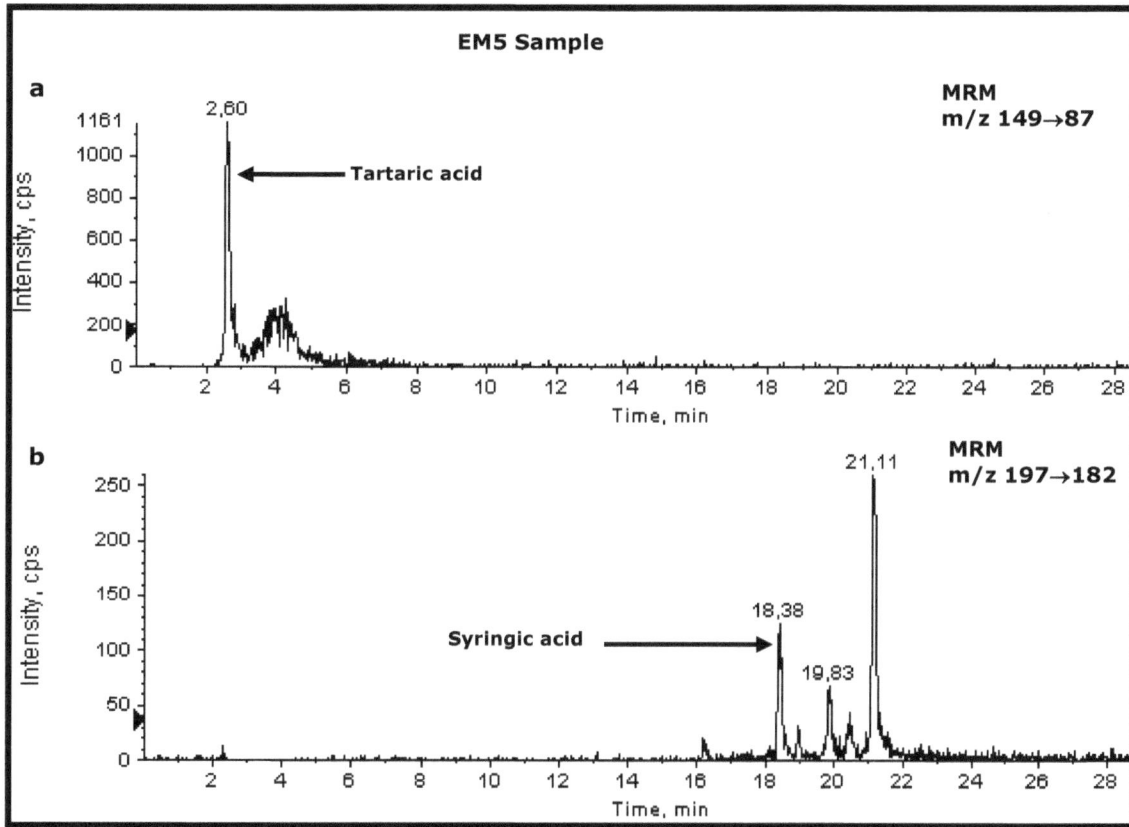

Figure L: LC/MS/MS chromatograms in MRM mode for the EM5 sample of residue from the amphora JE 62314 found beside the west wall at the Burial chamber of Tutankhamun's tomb [KV 62] in Western Thebes. (a) The grape marker tartaric acid is identified in the sample. (b) After performing alkaline fusion to the sample, the red grape marker syringic acid, derived from malvidin-3-glucoside, is also identified.

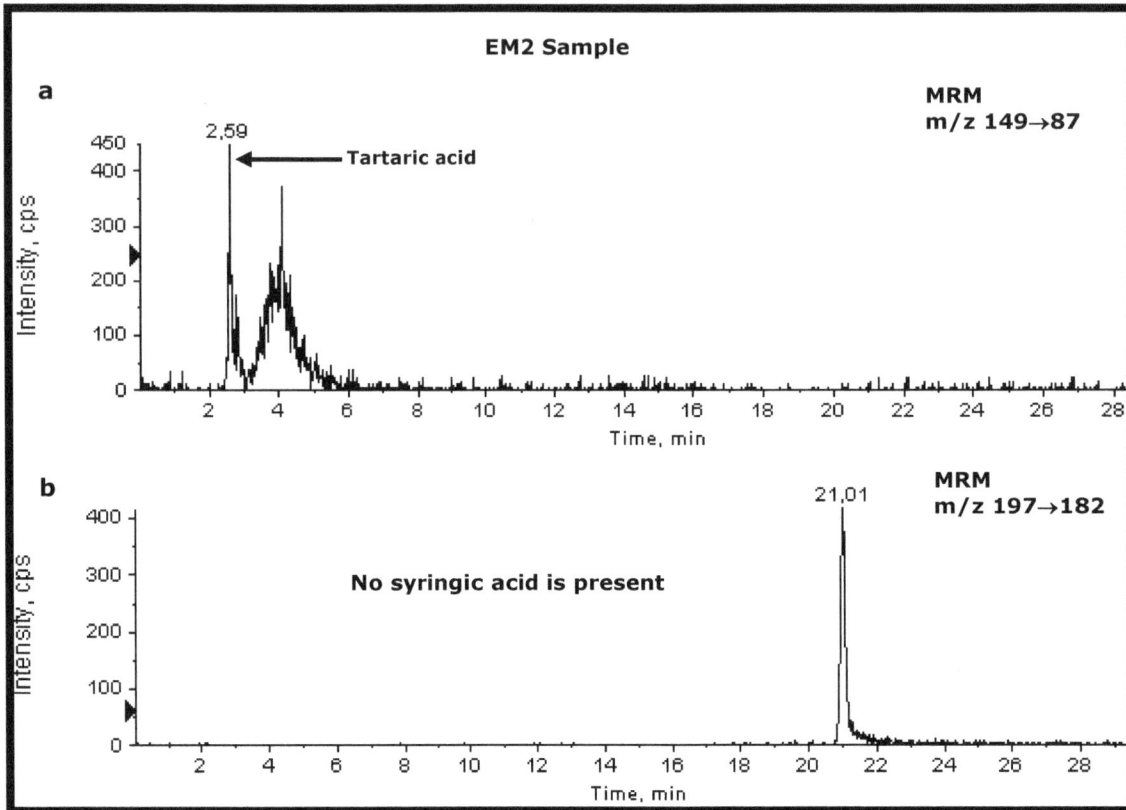

Figure M: LC/MS/MS chromatograms in MRM mode for the EM2 sample from the amphora JE 62302 inscribed "Visir Pentu". (a) The grape marker tartaric acid is identified in the sample. (b) After performing alkaline fusion to the sample, syringic acid derived from malvidin is not detected.

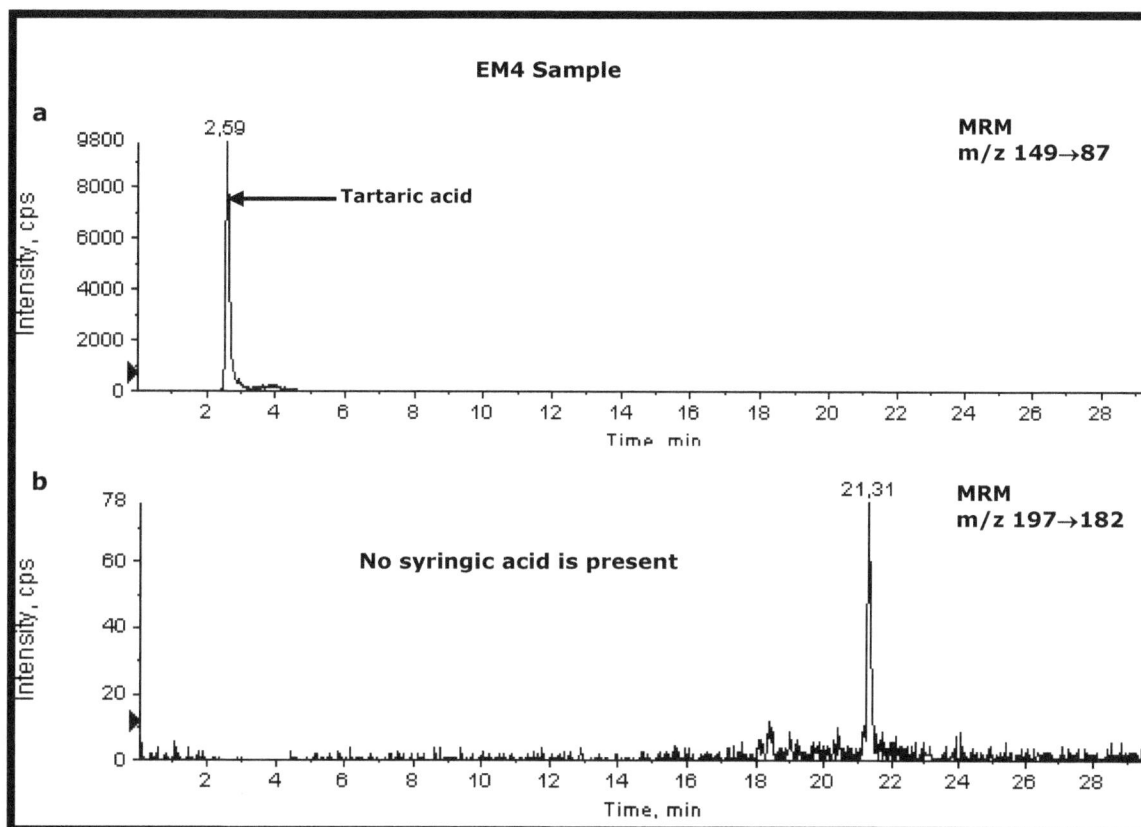

Figure N: LC/MS/MS chromatograms in MRM mode for the EM4 sample from the amphora JE 62312 inscribed "Sweet wine". (a) The grape marker tartaric acid is identified in the sample. (b) After performing alkaline fusion to the sample, syringic acid derived from malvidin-3-glucoside is not detected in the sample.

potassium hydroxide pellets. The extracts were injected in the LC/MS/MS system in the multiple reaction monitoring [MRM] mode, used as it is the most sensitive MS method.

The first investigation carried out was for tartaric acid, the marker characteristic for grapes. On the MRM chromatograms at the m/z 149→87 transition for tartaric acid [M_w 150], a peak of tartaric acid with the same retention time of the standard injected in the same conditions, was identified in all the samples. The results confirm the samples of residues EM1, EM2, EM3, EM4, EM5 and EM6 came from grapes.

Secondly, syringic acid as a red wine marker derived from the main red wine pigment malvidin-3-glucoside was investigated for, before and after performing the alkaline reaction. By using the MRM mode at the m/z 197→182 transition for syringic acid [M_w 198], a peak of syringic acid at the same retention time of the standard was identified in the EM5 sample after the alkaline reaction [Figure L]. No peak appeared before the alkaline reaction, syringic acid being, therefore released from malvidin-3-glucoside in the complex pigment. These results indicate that red grapes were the source for EM5 sample.

No syringic acid was detected before and after the alkaline reaction in the rest of samples: EM1, EM2

[see Figure M], EM3, EM4 [see Figure N]) and EM6.

Due to the different colour observed in these samples which was yellow-brownish, in contrast to the EM5 sample [dark-blackish] and the two samples previously studied (Guasch-Jané *et al*, 2004 and 2006A) in which red wine can be affirmed, and considering that tartaric acid and no syringic acid was found, we propose a white wine, as no marker for a white wine can be established and both the analysis and the hue point to it.

Discussion

The results of this research allow to assure that white wines [EM1, EM2, EM3, EM4 and EM6 samples] together with red wines [EM5 sample] were made in ancient Egypt at the end of the Eighteenth Dynasty, bearing the name *Irp*.

A detailed study of the inscriptions with respect to the results obtained shows that red wine [EM5 sample] and white wine [samples EM1, EM3 and EM4] were made at Western Delta in the estates owned by the Aten temple, near modern Alexandria. Moreover, the results indicate that in Tutankhamun's estate in the "Western River" a white wine [sample from amphora EM6] as well a red wine, sample previously reported in Guasch-

Jané *et al.* (2004), were made during the fifth year of Tutankhamun's reign.

Moreover, the results allow to affirm that the amphora labelled sweet wine [EM4 sample] was a white wine. Furthermore, a white wine was also contained in the amphora EM2 which was a present given to Tutankhamun by vizier Pentu, who may be present in the funerary procession on the east wall at the Burial chamber (Reeves, 1990). This may indicate that white wine was highly valued in Egypt since only the best products were offered for the afterlife of the Pharaoh.

Interestingly, the results allow us to reveal that a wine jar [EM5 sample] placed on the west wall of the Burial chamber contained a red wine, whose inscription states that it was made during the 9th year of Tutankhamun's reign by the vintner Sennufe in the Estate of Aten. In contrast to this, the EM6 sample from the amphora placed on the east wall, from the 5th year of the Estate of Tutankhamun made by vintner Khaa, was a white wine. Both wines came from the same Western River area.

Importantly, a red and a white wine were strategically placed surrounding Tutankhamun's body in the Burial chamber, together with a *Shedeh* amphora, the red wine located on the west and the white wine on the east. In contrast, all the objects found in the Annexe, which was intended as a store-room for oils, unguents, food and wines, were found in confusion with an overflow of other material belonging to the burial equipment (Reeves, 1990). If we consider that established rituals were performed by the Egyptian priests for the Pharaoh's burial and, according to Poo (1995), they organised and established the norms of religious texts and practices, then the real sense of the location of these two wine jars, both being next to the royal body, might have a particular symbolism with respect to rebirth.

Conclusions

The presence of white wine in ancient Egypt is reported here for the first time through the analysis of residue samples from Tutankhamun's amphorae using the LC/MS/MS method for the identification of wine markers. The results reveal that red and white wines were made at the Western Delta during the New Kingdom period, on the estates owned by the Aten temple and the king. Moreover, this research reveals that a red and a white wine were placed in Tutankhamun's Burial chamber, at the west and east side respectively. They might have had a special purpose for rebirth that needs investigation in-depth.

III.6. DISCUSSION

First of all, we shall comment on the new analytical method, secondly on the study of the colour of wine, then we shall investigate the source of *Shedeh* and finally the symbolism of wine in ancient Egypt will be considered.

III.6.1. THE ANALYTICAL METHOD

The second goal of this investigation was to demonstrate whether an amphora had contained wine or not. Up to now, all analytical methods dealing with identification of tartaric acid as a wine marker in archaeological samples had neither enough sensitivity nor good selectivity. Moreover, a huge quantity of sample was needed and, in some cases, the pottery fragment had to even be submerged in a solvent. Working with archaeological samples requires very sensitive methods to minimise the amount of sample to be used, as often only a very small quantity is available for analysis. When you work with catalogued material from museum collections you cannot take the object with you for analysis; at most, an authorization can be given to extract a small portion of its interior provided that there is something inside.

Neither did the previously published methods guarantee a good selectivity when identifying tartaric acid nor did they allow a study about the colour of wine, because tartaric acid and the other components identified by these methods do not give us information about what kind of grape has been used.

Therefore, it was necessary to develop a new highly sensitive method with a good specificity that would allow us to detect tartaric acid in very small quantities of sample, at a level of μg/L [ppb].

When it came to designing and validating the method for the identification of wine markers in archaeological residues, it was necessary to consider the quantity available and the physical characteristics of each sample. It must be considered that archaeological samples are not identical as, apart form their different origin, they evolve through time.

With the aim of identifying tartaric acid both in residues themselves and in dust obtained from scratching pottery, the liquid chromatography coupled with mass spectrometry [LC/MS/MS] technique was selected. The LC/MS/MS technique provides a high sensitivity when working with a low detection limit [ppb], and allows identification based on retention time and fragmentation pattern of the compound.

A disadvantage when using the liquid chromatography was that tartaric acid is a very polar compound and it does not get retained by reversed phase columns. However, this kind of column is broadly used for the identification of

syringic acid. After having tested several columns for the analysis of both polar and non polar compounds, the best option was found to be the Atlantis [Waters] column, with a reversed phase and optimised to work with 100% water mobile phases which are needed to identify tartaric acid. This column avoids dewetting caused by repulsion of the mobile phase in the silica pore, thing that would prevent migration of the analite to the pores and would make the analite pass through the column without retention. The optimum density of the ligands of this column, without an embedded polar group, provides strong retention of polar compounds without an excessive retention of non-polar compounds, in a way that the two compounds can be identified at the same time.

Given the high sensitivity of the method suggested -it has a detection limit of 0,05 μg/L-, we were able to study all samples working in MRM mode that gives the highest sensitivity thanks to the *m/z* 149→87 transition for tartaric acid and the *m/z* 197→182 transition for syringic acid.

First of all, the new method was applied to determine tartaric acid in samples from the following amphorae: British Museum num. EA 32684 and EA 59774, and the amphora Cairo Museum num. JE 57356. The first two were obtained by scraping the actual pottery and the third was a thin incrustation on the inner wall of the amphora. Besides, a sample was also scraped of the pink jar British Museum num. EA 51187 and studied.

Tartaric acid was identified in the first three samples [EA 32684, EA 59774 and JE 57356] and the results were compared with a blank that worked as a sample control. The blank was obtained by scrapping the outer side of a New Kingdom Egyptian pottery fragment. The results confirm that the amphorae from the British Museum num. EA 32684, EA 59774 and the amphora from the Cairo Museum num. JE 57356 contained wine indeed. Tartaric acid was not detected in the sample coming from the pink jar [EA 51187], which was thus not catalogued as a wine jar.

Secondly, the methodology was applied to the seven dry residue samples found inside Tutankhamun's amphorae at the Cairo Museum [see Figure 5.2.] to verify the presence of tartaric acid. Six of these amphorae bear an inscription indicating that they contained wine [*Irp*]: Cairo Museum num. JE 62301, JE 62303, JE 62312, JE 62313, JE 62314 and JE 62316. The seventh one, Cairo Museum num. JE 62302, has only "Visir Pentu" inscribed on it. Positive results were obtained for all seven samples, fact that confirms that the content of all amphorae was wine.

III.6.2. STUDY OF THE COLOUR OF WINE

The third objective of this research is to study the colour of wine so as to learn whether the wine made by ancient Egyptians was red or white.

Each one of the seven sample residues was subject to an alkaline oxidation. The presence of syringic acid was tested before and after the oxidation of the samples. MRM mode was performed at the maximum sensitivity *m/z* 197→182 transition for syringic acid detection.

Syringic acid was identified after the oxidation but not before in two samples from the Egyptian Museum section 1 [see III.1.2. samples 5 and 6]. Both residues are brown in colour and come from amphorae Cairo Museum num. JE 62313 and JE 62314 respectively. Due to the fact that syringic acid was identified after oxidation, it can be affirmed that syringic acid came from malvidin in the polymeric structure formed over time. These results confirm that red wine existed in ancient Egypt during the New Kingdom period.

However, syringic acid was not detected in samples num. 1, 2, 3, 4 and 8 [see III.1.2.] which belong to amphorae Cairo Museum num. JE 62301, JE 62302, JE 62303, JE 62312 and JE 62316 respectively. In these dry residue samples, yellowish in colour, tartaric acid was identified so that we can affirm that their raw material was grape. We can conclude from the results that the wine these five amphorae contained was white.

Due to the lack of historical records about the colour of Egyptian wine, and having said that the only written information found on amphorae related to it is *Irp*, the results of this research allow to state that both kinds of wine, white and red, were included in Egyptian amphorae under the name *Irp*.

To sum up, we can affirm that from the seven amphorae chosen for this study, two of them contained red wine while the other five contained white wine, among which one was labelled as "sweet wine" [amphora JE 62312]. Furthermore, the amphora given by vizir Pentu to Tutankhamun contained also white wine. Concerning the two wine jars dating from the 5th year from the Estate of Aten in the Western River, it can be said that one of them [JE 62316] contained white wine while the other one [JE 62313] red wine.

III.6.3. INVESTIGATING THE *SHEDEH* SOURCE

The fourth goal we intended to achieve was to discover the raw material from which *Shedeh* was made. According to the Papyrus Salt 825 from the Late Period [712-332 BC], which is the only preserved text that describes the preparation of *Shedeh*, more than one filtration and heating period were needed to elaborate *Shedeh* (Derchain, 1965). Several hypotheses exist about what kind of beverage *Shedeh* was, and two of them still are under discussion on the kind of fruit used for the manufacture of *Shedeh*. The first hypothesis (Loret, 1892) proposed that it could be

pomegranate wine; this supposition is wide spread, in a way that it can be found in relatively recent bibliography. However, it is questionable because it is based on an association of words and it does not take the fragment of Papyrus Salt 825 just mentioned into consideration. The second hypothesis about the origin of *Shedeh* suggests that it could be grape wine but elaborated following a different procedure than that of traditional wine (Erman, 1930). According to Tallet (1995), it was cooked wine. This hypothesis at least considers the procedure the Papyrus Salt 825 describes: heating.

With the aim of confirming which of these hypotheses was right, a different point of view was considered: the analysis of a sample of a residue from a *Shedeh* amphora.

There are not many amphorae inscribed with the word *Shedeh* that are in a good state of conservation because the earliest inscriptions appear at the middle of Dynasty 18th [second half of the 14th century BC] and they disappear at the end of the Ramessid Period [about 12th century BC]. Only fifteen *Shedeh* inscriptions have been documented (Tallet, 1995). Most of them are amphora fragments and thus there is no deposit residue left. Three out of the fifteen *Shedeh* inscriptions are inscribed on amphorae found in the tomb of Tutankhamun, and housed nowadays at the Egyptian Museum in Cairo; they come from an intact context closed for more than 3.330 years. Among these three amphorae, the only one which is complete -although opened on its upper part-, was found inside the intact burial chamber: the amphora Cairo Museum num. JE 62315 [see Figure 6.2.].

The analysis of the residue sample coming from amphora JE 62315 allowed us to identify tartaric acid, as well as syringic acid after sample oxidation confirming that it came from malvidin. These results reveal that *Shedeh* was made from red grapes and accordingly it can be said that *Shedeh* was red wine with a more elaborate manufacture process.

III.6.4. THE SYMBOLISM OF WINE

As mentioned above, ancient Egyptians did not record the colour of wine in texts or inscribed amphorae. From this, it could be inferred that the type of wine was of no importance for Egyptians when, being so meticulous in documenting as they were, they never made any reference to it. However, the results of this research reveil that there was even an established symbolism behind the colour of wine. In the Burial chamber of Tutankhamun, an amphora with red wine of the 9th vintage year from the Estate of Aten of the Western River was placed beside the west wall, between the wall and the sarcophagus housing the mummy of the pharaoh. On the east side, another amphora contained white wine. According to the inscription, it was wine of the 5th year coming from the Estate of Tutankhamun in the Western River.

The fact that one of the amphorae in the Burial chamber contained white wine and the other one red manifests the great importance that the colour of wine would have had for ancient Egyptians and it raises, at the same time, the question of why white wine would had been placed in the east while red wine in the west. All recorded information regarding symbolism of wine is based on the red colour. That is, without any doubt, because of the relation established between the blood of Osiris, the God of death and resurrection who, according to Egyptian beliefs was the first one of the Westerns [=Deaths], and red wine also

associated with the colour of the Nile when the fertilising flood occurred. For this reason, the amphora containing red wine would have been placed on the west side of the Burial chamber. But what is the reason why an amphora containing white wine was placed next to the east wall? Was it only because white wine was not allowed to indicate the west direction inside the Burial chamber? If that had been the case, placing red wine in the west would have been enough. But it must be remembered that nothing was left to chance and that the priests who were in charge of the burial of the pharaoh performed the funeral rituals of their time to perfection.

IV. CONCLUSIONS

The conclusions drawn from this study are the following:

1. From an analytical point of view, verifying the presence of wine through the identification of tartaric acid in archaeological samples [both scrapings from the pottery and dry deposit residues] has been proved effective thanks to a new method of analysis that uses the LC/MS/MS technique. The quantity needed for analysis is only 2 mg.

   ✧ Tartaric acid has been detected in the following Egyptian amphorae: British Museum num. EA 32684 and EA 59774 and also in amphora Cairo Museum num. JE 57356 and, consequently, it can be stated that these three amphorae did contain wine.

2. During the 18th Dynasty Egypt [1.543-1.292 BC], both white and red wine were comprised under the same name: *Irp*.

   ✧ The presence of both tartaric and syringic acid has been identified in dry brownish residue samples found inside Egyptian amphorae belonging to Tutankhamun's collection: Cairo Museum num. JE 62313 and JE 62314 allowing us to confirm that both contained wine manufactured from red grapes.

   ✧ While tartaric acid has been identified in dry residue samples, of a yellowish colour, which came from amphorae Cairo Museum num. JE 62301, JE 62302, JE 62303, JE 62312 and JE 62316, no syringic acid was detected. Therefore, we can assert that the liquid contained in these five amphoras was white wine.

3. Thanks to the identification of not only tartaric but also syringic acid in a black sample of a dry residue extracted from the *Shedeh* amphora Cairo Museum num. JE 62315, we can affirm that red grape was the botanical source of *Shedeh,* drink that was kept in wine-jar-like amphorae with inscriptions.

The contributions of the study are:

⚭ The analytical method developed during this PhD research, using liquid chromatography coupled to mass spectrometry in tandem [LC/MS/MS], is suitable for the study of archaeological samples thanks to its high sensitivity and selectivity and, besides, it allowed for the first time the identification of two compound wine markers in archaeology: tartaric acid and syringic acid released from malvidin.

⚭ It has been first demonstrated that, through an alkaline oxidation, syringic acid -coming from malvidin, found in grapes and young red wine- can be released from the complex polymer formed over time and it can be established as a red grape marker in archaeological residues.

⚭ The mystery of the origins of *Shedeh* has been solved and the fact that Egyptian enological specialization was transmited to other Mediterranean cultures up to the present time has been revealed. This research establishes the existence of three kinds of grape products in ancient Egypt: white wine, red wine and a more elaborate red wine, named *Shedeh* by ancient Egyptians.

⚭ The possibility to study the symbolism behind the colour of wine has emerged from this research providing an unhindered opportunity for historians and archaeologists to investigate the role of white wine in the ancient Egyptian civilization.

V. APPENDICES

V.1. MAP OF EGYPT

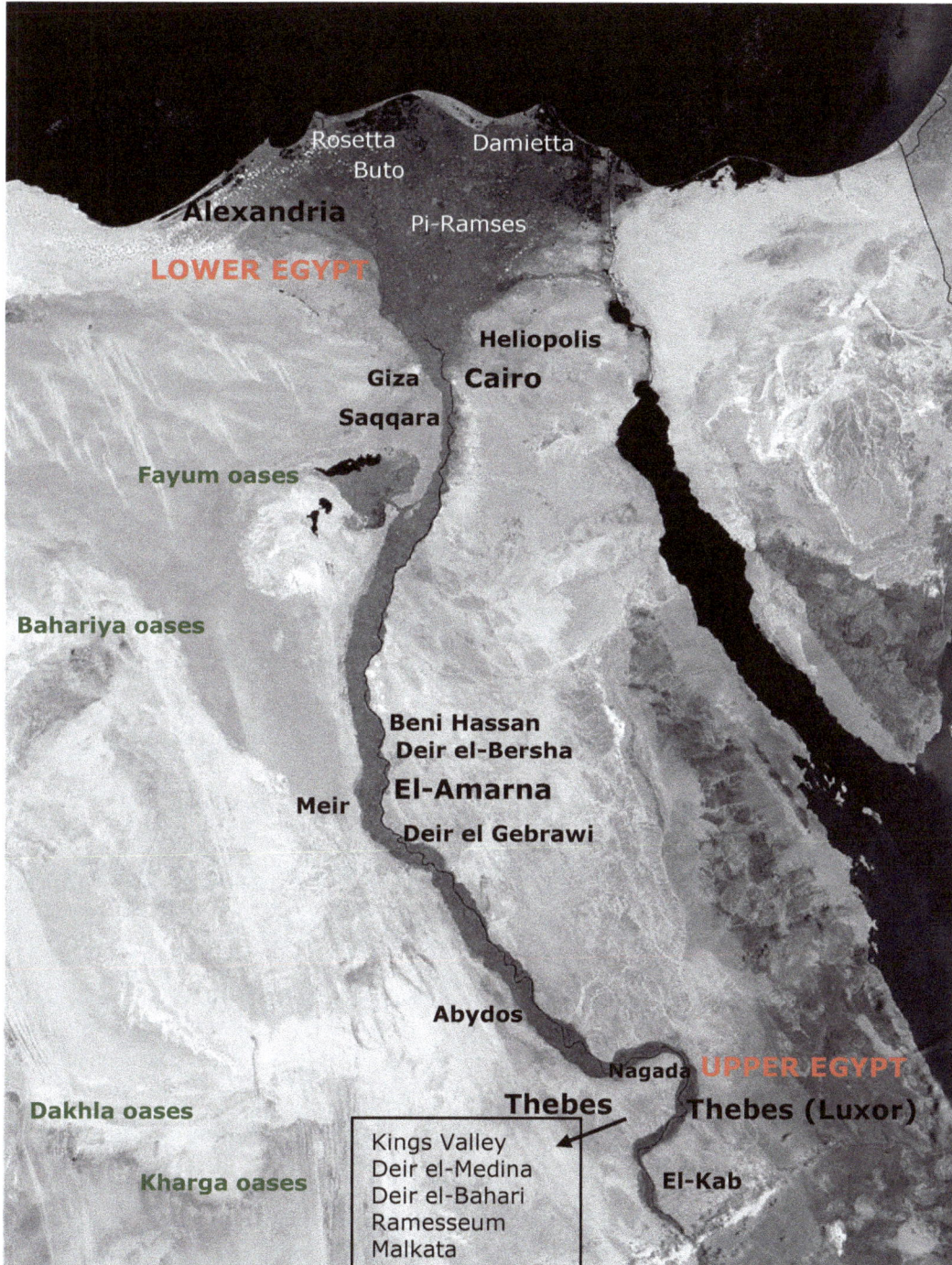

V.2. CHRONOLOGY OF ANCIENT EGYPT

Historical periods with corresponding approximate dates (Baines and Malek, 2002), as cited in the book.

PREDYNASTIC: 4.000-3.150 BC
   ***Nagada I** (4.000-3.500 BC)
   Nagada II and III (3.500-3.150 BC)

DYNASTIC PERIOD
   ¤ **Early Dynastic: 2.950-2.575 BC**
      1st Dynasty^ (2.950-2.775 BC)
      2nd Dynasty (2.775-2.650 BC)
      3rd Dynasty (2.650-2.575 BC)

   ¤ **Old Kingdom: 2.575-2.150 BC**
      4th Dynasty (2.575-2.450 BC)
      5th Dynasty (2.450-2.325 BC)
      6th Dynasty (2.325-2.175 BC)
      7th/8th Dynasty (2.175-2.125 BC)

   ¤ **First Intermediate period: 2.125-1.975BC**
      9th Dynasty (2.125-2.080 BC)
         (Herakleopolitan)
      10th Dynasty (2.080-1.975 BC)
         (Herakleopolitan)
      11th Dynasty (2.080-1.975 BC)
         (Theban)

   ¤ **Middle Kingdom: 1.975-1.640 BC**
      11th Dynasty (1.975-1.940 BC)
         (all Egypt)
      12th Dynasty (1.938-1.775 BC)
      13th Dynasty (1.775-1.630 BC)
      14th Dynasty (contemporaneous with the 13th-15th Dynasties)

   ¤ **Second Intermediate period: 1.630-1.520 BC**
      15th Dynasty (1.630-1.520 BC) **(Hyksos)**
      16th Dynasty (Hyksos, contemporaneous with 15th the Dynasty)
      17th Dynasty (1.630-1.540 BC)

   ¤ **New Kingdom: 1.539-1.075 BC**
      18th Dynasty (1.539-1.292 BC)
      —Amarna Period (late 18th Dyn.): from Akhenaten to Tutankhamun
      19th Dynasty (1.292-1.190 BC)
      — Ramessid Period
      20th Dynasty (1.190-1.075 BC)
      —Ramessid Period

   ¤ **Third Intermediate period: 1.075-715 BC**
      21th Dynasty (1.075-945 BC)
      22th Dynasty (945-715 BC)
      23th Dynasty (830-715 BC)
      24th Dynasty (730-715 BC)
         (Sais)
      25th Dynasty (770-715 BC)

- ¤ **Late period: 715-332 BC**
  25th Dynasty (715-657 BC)
  (Nubia and all Egypt)
  26th Dynasty (664-525 BC)
  27th Dynasty (525-404 BC)
  (Persian)
  28th Dynasty (404-399 BC)
  29th Dynasty (399-380 BC)
  30th Dynasty (380-343 BC)
  2nd Persian period (343-332 BC)

- ¤ **Greco-Roman period: 332 BC- 395**
  Macedonian Dynasty (332-305 BC)
  Ptolemaic Dynasty (305-30 BC)
  Roman Emperors (30 BC-395)

*Nagada: Site that gives name to three different stages of cultural development in Upper and Lower Egypt, before the unification of the land.

^Dynasty: Temporary period during which Egypt is considered an unified land, and comprising each one of them a series of reigns. They are numbered from the 1st to the 30th dynasty.

V.3. ABBREVIATIONS

CATALOGUE FROM THE EGYPTIAN MUSEUM IN CAIRO:
    JE= number of the *Journal d'Entrée*
    C= either Carter's number, excavation's number or object's number
    G= *Guide* number or Exhibition number
    SR= *Special Register* number

CATALOGUE FROM THE DEPARTMENT OF ANCIENT EGYPT AND SUDAN, BRITISH MUSEUM, LONDON:
    EA= *Egyptian Archaeology*

l.p.h.= Life, prosperity and health. It is a common Egyptian formula.
D. O.= Spanish Wine's Origin Denomination.

TOMBS IN WEST THEBES:
    TT: Theban Tomb
    KV: King's Valley tomb
    WV: Western's Valley tomb

VI. BIBLIOGRAPHY

Atanasova V., Fulcrand H., Cheynier V. and Moutounet M. "Effect of oxygenation on polyphenol changes occurring in the course of wine-making." Analytica Chimica Acta 458 (2002): 15-27.

Athenaeus (I, 33 d-f): "Athenaeus. The Deipnosophists." Translated by C.B. Gulick. Seven volumes. Loeb Classical Library. Hardvard University Press. London, 1927-1941.

Badler V.R., McGovern P.E. and Michel R.H. "Drink and be Merry! Infrared spectroscopy and ancient near Eastern wine." MASCA Research Papers in Science and Archaeology 7 (1990): 25-36.

Baines J. and Malek J. "Cultural Atlas of Ancient Egypt." Andromeda Oxford Limited. The American University in Cairo Press. Cairo, 2002: p. 12-18, 36-37.

Bakker J. and Timberlake C.F. "Isolation, identification and characterization of new color-stable anthocyanins occurring in some red wines." Journal of Agricultural and Food Chemistry 45 (1997): 35-43.

Barguet P. "Le Livre des Morts des Anciens Égyptiens." Éditions du Cerf. Paris, 1967: p. 234-235.

Baum N. "Arbres et Arbustes de l'Egypte Ancienne." Orientalia Lovaniensia Analecta 31. Leuven, 1988: p. 135-148.

Beinlich, H. and Saleh, M. "Corpus der Hieroglyphischen Inschriften aus dem Grab des Tutanchamun: mit Konkordanz der Nummernsysteme des Journal d'Entrée des Ägyptischen Museums Kairo, der Handlist to Howard Carter's Catalogue of Objects in Tutankhamun's Tomb un der Ausstellungs-Nummer des Ägyptischen Museums Kairo". Griffith Institute. Oxford, 1989: p. 246.

Berget, A. Chronique d'Égypte IX, 1934: p. 221-224.

Blackman A.M. "The Rock Tombs of Meir, Volume III" Archaeological Survey of Egypt. Twenty-Fourth Memoir. Egypt Exploration Society. London, 1915: p. 30.

Blackman A.M. and Apted M.R. "The Rock Tombs of Meir, Volume V." Archaeological Survey of Egypt. Twenty-Eight Memoir. Egypt Exploration Society. London, 1953: Plate XX.

Brunner, H. "Granatapfel" in "Lexikon der Ägyptologie, Volume II" Harrassowitz. Wiesbaden, 1977: p. 891-892.

Carter H. "The Tomb of Tut.ankh.Amen Discovered by the Late Earl of Carnarvon and Howard Carter, Volume II". Cassell and Company Ltd. 1927. Reprinted by Reeves, N. "The Tomb of Tut.ankh.Amen 2: The Burial Chamber", Duckworth and Co. Ltd. Bath, 2001: p. 30.

Carter H. "The Tomb of Tut.ankh.Amen Discovered by the Late Earl of Carnarvon and Howard Carter, Volume III". Cassell & Company Ltd. 1933. Reprinted by N. Reeves. "The Tomb of Tut.ankh.Amen: The Annexe and Treasury", Duckworth and Co. Ltd. Bath, 2000: p. 144-150.

Carter, Archaeological cards in "Tutankhamun: Anatomy of an Excavation. The Howard Carter Archives." Griffith Institute. Oxford, 2000-2003. http://www.ashmol.ox.ac.uk//gri/carter

Carter N° 206, in "Tutankhamun: Anatomy of an Excavation, The Howard Carter Archives." Griffith Institute. Oxford, 2000-2003. http://www.ashmol.ox.ac.uk//gri/carter/206-c206-2.html

Černý J. "Chapter I. Wine-jars" in "Hieratic Inscriptions from the Tomb of Tutankhamun." Tutankhamun's Tomb Series II. Ed. John Baines. Griffith Institute. Oxford, 1965: pp 1-4.

Černý J. "Three Regnal Dates of the Eighteen Dynasty." Journal of Egyptian Archaeology (JEA) 50 (1964): 37-39.

Cervelló J. "Egipto y África. Origen de la Civilización y la Monarquía Faraónicas en su Contexto Africano" Aula Orientalis Suplementa, 13. Editorial Ausa. Barcelona, 1996: p. 216-218.

Chassinat E. "Le Mistère d'Osiris au Mois de Khoiak, Volume II." Institut Français d'Archéologie Orientale (IFAO). Le Caire, 1968: p. 788-793.

Cherpion N. "Deux Tombes de la XVIIIe Dynastie à Deir El-Medina: n° 340 (Amenemhat) et 354 (anonime)." Mémoires de l'Institut Français d'Archeologie Orientale (MIFAO) 114. Cairo, 1999: p. 24-26, 95-97.

Condamin J. and Formenti F. "Recherche de traces d'huile d'olive et de vin." Figlina 1 (1976): 143-158.

Condamin J. and Formenti F. "Detecció du contenu d'amphores antiques (huiles, vin). Étude methodologique." Revue d'Archéométrie 2 (1978): 43-58.

Davies N. de G. "The Mastaba of Ptahhotep and Akhethotep at Saqqara. Part I: The Chapel and the Hieroglyphs." Archaeological Survey of Egypt. Eighth Memoir. Egypt Exploration Fund. London, 1900.

Davies N. de G. "The Rock Tombs of Deir El-Gebrâwi. Part II: Tomb of Zau and Tombs of Northern Group." Archaeological Survey of Egypt. Twelfth Memoir. Special Publication of the Egypt Exploration Fund. London, 1902.

Davies N. de G. "The Rock Tombs of El-Amarna. Part III: The tombs of Huya and Ahmes." Archaeological Survey of Egypt. Ed. F.Ll Griffith. Egypt Exploration Fund. London, 1905: Pl. VI, VIII.

Davies N. de G. "The Rock Tombs of El-Amarna. Part IV: The tombs of Pentu, Mahu and others." Archaeological Survey of Egypt. Ed. F.Ll Griffith. Egypt Exploration Fund. London, 1906: Pl. II.

Davies N. de G. "The Rock Tombs of El-Amarna. Part VI: The tombs of Parennefer, Tutu and Ay." Archaeological Survey of Egypt. Ed. F.Ll Griffith. Egypt Exploration Fund. London, 1908: Pl. IV.

Derchain P. "Le Papyrus Salt 825 (B.M. 10051): Rituel pour la Conservation de la Vie en Égypte." Mémoires LVIII. Académie Royale de Belgique. Bruxelles, 1965: p. 137 (II,1) and 147-149 (n.10).

Desroches-Noblecourt C. "Vie et Mort d'un Pharaon. Toutankhamon." Hachette. Paris, 1963: p. 204.

Desroches-Noblecourt C. and Kuenz Ch. "Le Petit Temple d'Abou Simbel." Ministère de la Culture. Centre de Documentation et Étude sur L'Ancienne Égypte. Mémoires I. Le Caire, 1968: p. 116, 122; Pl. CV, CXIII.

Desroches-Noblecourt C. "La Tombe aux Vignes." Fondation Kodak-Pathé. Paris, 1985: p. 9.

Desroches-Noblecourt C. "Amours et Fureurs de La Lointaine." Stock-Pernoud. Paris, 1995: p. 37-45.

Eaton-Krauss M. "Tutanchamun" in "Lexikon der Ägyptologie VI". Harrassowitz. Wiesbaden, 1986: p. 812-816.

El-Khouli A., Holthoer R., Hope C. and Kaper O.E. "Stone Vessels, Pottery and Sealings from the Tomb of Tutankhamun". Ed. John Baines. Griffith Institute. Oxford, 1993: Fig. B, Pl. 26-32.

Emery W.B. "Archaic Egypt." London, 1961: p. 121, 127.

Erman A. and Grapow H. "Wörterbuch der Ägyptischen Sprache", 5 volumes. Akademie Verlag. Hinrichs. Leipzig, 1926-31.
   Irp: Wörterbuch I, 1926: p. 115.
   Šdḥ: Wörterbuch IV, 1930: p. 568.

Faulkner R.O. "The Ancient Egyptian Pyramid Texts". Oxford University Press. Oxford, 1969: p. 30 (Utterances 153-157).

Fulcrand H., Benabdeljalil C., Rigaud J., Cheynier V. and Moutounet M. "A new class of wine pigments generated by reaction between pyruvic acid and grape anthocyanins." Phytochemistry 47 (1998): 1401-1407.

Gabolde M. "La Postérité d'Aménophis III". Egyptes, I (1993): p. 29-34.

Gabolde M. "D'Akhenaton à Toutankhamon". Collection de l'Institut d'Archéologie et d'Histoire de l'Antiquité, Volume 3. Université Lumière-Lyon 2. Paris, 1998: p. 1-2, 123, 161, 219-221.

Gardiner A.H. "VIII. Beverages: *Šdḥ* (n.564)" in "Ancient Egyptian Onomastica, Volume II". Oxford University Press. Oxford, 1947, p. 235.

Gardiner A.H. "Egyptian Grammar". 3rd Edition, revised. Griffith Institute. Oxford, 1994.

Garnier N., Cren-Olivé C., Rolando C. and Regert M. "Characterization of archaeological beeswax by electron ionization and electrospray ionization mass spectrometry". Analytical Chemistry 74 (2002): 4868-4877.

Garnsey, P. "Food and Society in Classical Antiquity". Cambridge University Press. Cambridge, 1999.

Girard, P.S. "Description de l'Égypte, état moderne, Volume II." Mémoire sur l'agriculture, l'industrie et le commerce de l'Égypte. Paris, 1812: p. 608.

Guasch-Jané M.R., Ibern-Gómez M., Andrés-Lacueva C., Jáuregui O. and Lamuela-Raventós R.M. "Liquid chromatography with mass spectrometry in tandem mode applied for the identification of wine markers in residues from ancient Egyptian vessels". Analytical Chemistry 76 (2004): 1672-1677.

Guasch-Jané M.R., Andrés-Lacueva C., Jáuregui O. and Lamuela-Raventós R.M. "The origin of the ancient Egyptian drink *shedeh* revealed using LC/MS/MS". Journal of Archaeological Science 33 (2006 A): 98-101.

Guasch-Jané M.R., Andrés-Lacueva C., Jáuregui O. and Lamuela-Raventós R.M. "First evidence of white wine in ancient Egypt from Tutankhamun's tomb". Journal of Archaeological Science 33 (2006 B): 1075-1080.

Helck W. "Getränke" in "Lexikon der Ägyptologie, Volume II". Harrassowitz. Wiesbaden, 1977: p. 585-586.

Holthoer R. "The Pottery" in "Stone Vessels, Pottery and Sealings from the Tomb of Tutankhamun". Ed. John Baines. Griffith Institute. Oxford, 1993: p. 39-85.

Hope C.A. "Jar Sealings and Amphorae of the 18th Dynasty: A Technological Study. Excavations at Malkata and the Birket Habu 1971-1974. Egyptology Today 2, volume V. Aris and Phillips Ltd. Warminster, 1978: p. 6-7, 14-15.

Hope C.A. "The Jar Sealings" in "Stone Vessels, Pottery and Sealings from the Tomb of Tutankhamun". Ed. John Baines. Griffith Institute. Oxford, 1993: p. 89-136.

ICH guidelines: "The International Conference on Harmonization of Technical Requirements for the Registration of Drugs for Human Use." Validation of Analytical Procedures. Geneve, Switzerland, May 1997. www.ich.org

James T.G.H. "The earliest History of Wine and its importance in ancient Egypt" in "The origins and Ancient History of Wine." Gordon and Breach Publishers. Amsterdam, 1996: p. 197-213.

James T.G.H. "Howard Carter, The Path to Tutankhamun." The American University in Cairo Press, Cairo, 2001: p. 22-44.

Janssen J.J. "Commodity Prices from the Ramessid Period. An Economic Study of the Village of Necropolis Workmen at Thebes" E.J. Brill. Leiden, 1975: p. 350-353.

Johnson H. "Une Histoire Mondiale du Vin de l'Antiquité à nos Jours." Hachette. Paris, 1989: p. 24-34.

Keimer L. "Gartenpflanzen im Alten Ägypten." Deutsches Archäologisches Instituts Abteilung Kairo (DAIK), Volume I. Hambourg, 1924: p. 152.

Kemp B.J. "Ancient Egypt: Anatomy of a Civilization." Rouledge. London, 1989: p. 368-370.

Khoemoth P. "Osiris et les Arbres. Contribution à l'Étude des Arbres Sacrés de l'Égypte Ancienne." Aegyptiaca Leodinensia 3. Liège, 1994: p. 241-245.

Lerstrup A. "The making of wine in Egypt." Göttinger Miszellen 129: 61-82.

Lesko L.H. "King Tut's Wine Cellar." BC Scribe Publications. California, 1977.

Lesko, L.H. "Egyptian Wine Production during the New Kingdom" in "The Origins and Ancient History of Wine". Gordon and Breach Publishers. Amsterdam, 1996: p. 215-230.

"Lexikon der Ägyptologie" (LÄ), Band I-VI. Helck W. and Westendorf W., Eds. Harrassowitz. Wiesbaden, 1977-1986.

    Getranke: LÄ II, 1977: p. 585-586.

    Granatapfel: LÄ II, 1977: p. 891-892.

    Wein: LÄ VI, 1986: p. 1169-1192.

Loret V. "La flore pharaonique". Ernest Leroux Ed. Paris, 1892: p. 76-78.

Lucas A. "Ancient Egyptian Materials and Industries". 4rd ed. Revised, J.R Harris. Edward Arnold. London, 1962: p. 18.

Macheix, J.J., Fleuriet, A. and Billot, J. Fruit Phenolics, CRC Press. Boca Ratón, Florida, 1990: p. 41-57.

Martin G.T. "The Hidden Tombs of Memphis." Thames and Hudson Ltd. London, 1991: p. 147.

Mateus N., Pascual-Teresa S., Rivas-Gonzalo J.C., Santos-Buelga, C. and de Freitas V. "Structural diversity of anthocyanin-derived pigments in Port wines." Food Chemistry 76 (2002): 335-342.

Mathieu B. "La Poésie Amoureuse de l'Égypte Ancienne. Chapitre II: La Collection du Papyrus Harris 500, R° (P.BM 10060)." Bibliothèque d'Étude 115. Institut Français d'Archeologie Orientale. Cairo, 1996: p. 64, 75 (n. 220) and 79 (n. 258).

Mc Govern P.E., Glusker D.L., Exner L.J. and Voig M.M. "Neolithic resinated wine." Nature 381 (1996): 480-481.

Meeks D. "Oléiculture et viticulture dans l'Égypte pharaonique". Bulletin de Correspondance Hellénique Supplement XXVI. Ecole Français d'Athenes. Athens, 1993: p. 3-38.

Meeks D. and Favard-Meeks C. "Daily Life of the Egyptian Gods". Translated from French by G.M. Goshgarian. Cornell University Press. London, 1996: p. 118.

Menguin O. and Amer M. "The Excavations of the Egyptian University in the Neolithic Site of the Maadi: First Preliminary Report". Cairo, 1932.

Mercer S.A.B. "The Pyramid Texts in Translation and Commentary." Volume 1. Longmans Green and Co. New York-London-Toronto, 1952: p. 48-49.

Meyer Ch. "Wein" in "Lexikon der Ägyptologie VI". Harrassowitz. Wiesbaden, 1986: 1169-1182.

Michel R.H., Mc Govern P.E. and Badler V.R. "The first wine and beer. Chemical Detection of Ancient Beverages." Analytical Chemistry 65 (1993): 408A-413A.

Montet P. "La Fabrication du Vin dans les Tombeaux Antérieurs au Nouvel Empire." Recueil de Travaux Relatifs a la Philologie et a l'Archéologie Égyptiennes et Assyriennes, 35. Paris, 1913: p. 117-124.

Moussa A.M. and Altenmüller H. "Das Grab des Nianchchnum und Chnumhotep." Phillip von Zabern. Mainz, 1977: Fig. 16.

Murray M.A. "Viticulture and wine production" in "Ancient Egyptian Materials and Technology." Nicholson P.T. and Shaw I. Eds., Cambridge University Press. Cambridge, 2000: p. 577-599.

Newberry P.E. "Beni Hassan. Part I." Archaeological Survey of Egypt. Published under the auspices of the Egypt Exploration Fund. London, 1893: Pl. XII, XXIX.

Newberry P.E. "Beni Hassan. Part II." Archaeological Survey of Egypt. Ed. F.Ll. Griffith. Published under the auspices of the Egypt Exploration Fund. London, 1894: Pl. VI, XVI.

Newberry P.E. "El Bersheh. Part I: The Tomb of Tehuti-Hotep." Archaeological Survey of Egypt. Special publication of the Egypt Exploration Fund. London, s.a.: Pl. XXVI.

Pavitt, N. "Africa's Great Rift Valley." Harry N. Abrams INC., Publishers. New York, 2001: p. 149.

Para, M.H. "Notre Histoire dans le Fond des Amphore. Determination des Acides Amines et des Acides Phenoliques en CLHP." Lyon, 1982.

Pendlebury, J.D.S. and Frankfort H. "City of Akhenaten" II. Egypt Exploration Society. Londres, 1933.

Poo, M.Ch. "Weinopfer" in "Lexikon der Ägyptologie VI". Harrassowitz. Wiesbaden, 1986: 1185-1190.

Poo, M.Ch. "Wine and Wine Offering in the Religion of Ancient Egypt". Kegan Paul Int. London, 1995: p. 13-14, 39, 53-54, 71, 148, 170.

Raventós, M. "La Verema." Barcelona, 1911: p. 93.

Reeves, N. "The Complete Tutankhamun." Thames and Hudson Ltd. London, 1990: p. 22, 24-25, 33, 48-49, 53, 70-74, 82-85, 89-97.

Säve-Söderbergh T. "Four Eighteenth Dynasty Tombs." Private Tombs at Thebes, 1. Griffith Institute. Oxford, 1957: Pl. XIV.

Shedid A.G. and Seidel M. "The Tomb of Nakht." Verlag Philipp von Zabern. Mainz am Rhein, 1996: p. 42 and 57.

Singleton V.L. "An Enologist's Commentary on Ancient Wines" in "The Origins and Ancient History of Wine." Gordon and Breach Publishers. Philadelphia, 1996: p. 67-77.

Sist, L. "L'Alimentazione nel Mondo Antico. Gli Egizi." Giornata Mondiale dell'Alimentazione, 16 Ottobre 1987. Ministero per i Beni Culturali e Ambientali. Instituto Poligrafico e Zecca dello Stato. Libreria dello Stato. Rome, 1987: p. 19-24.

Sleno L. and Volmer D.A. "Ion activation methods for tandem mass spectrometry". Journal of Mass Spectrometry 39 (2004): 1091-1112.

Somers T.C. "Wine tannins-isolation of condensed flavonoid pigments by gel-filtration." Nature 209 (1966): 368-370.

Stroudhal E. "Life of the Ancient Egyptians." The American University in Cairo Press. Cairo, 1992: p. 91, 93, 125-133.

Tallet P. "Le shedeh: étude d'un procédé de vinification en Égypte ancienne." Bulletin de l'Institut Français d'Archéologie Orientale (BIFAO) 95 (1995): 459-492.

Tallet P. "Quelques Aspects de l'Économie du Vin en Égypte Ancienne, au Nouvel Empire." A "Le Commerce en Égypte Ancienne." Ed. N. Grimal and B. Menu. Bibliothèque d'Étude 121. Institut Français d'Archéologie Orientale. Cairo, 1998: p. 241-263.

Taylor J.H. "The Tombs of the Kings", Chapter 5: "The threshold of Eternity: Tombs, Cemeteries and Mortuary Cults" in "Death and the Afterlife in Ancient Egypt." The British Museum Press. London, 2001: p. 141-147.

"The Cambridge World History of Food." K.F. Kiple and K.C. Ornelas, editors. Cambridge University Press. Cambridge, 2000.

Tylor J.J. and Griffith F.Ll. "The Tomb of Paheri at El Kab." Eleventh Memoir. Egypt Exploration Society. London, 1894: Pl. IV.

USP XXVIII: United States Pharmacopeia XXVIII. Validation of Compendial Methods 1225 (2005): 2748-2751.

Vandersleyen C. "L'Égypte et la Vallée du Nil. Tome 2: De la fin de l'Ancien Empire à la fin du Nouvel Empire." Nouvelle Clio. Presses Universitaires de France. Paris, 1995: p. 467-478.

Van Dijk J. "Hieratic inscriptions from the tomb of Maya at Saqqara: a preliminary survey." Göttinger Miszellen 127 (1992): 23-32.

Vandier J. "Manuel d'Archéologie Égyptienne, Volume I: Les Époques de Formation." Paris, 1952: p. 496.

Vansleb R.D. "The Present State of Egypt or a New Relation of a Late Voyage into That Kingdom (1672-1673)." J. Starkey. London, 1678.

Vercoutter J. "A la recherche de l'Égypte oubliée". Ed. Gallimard. Paris, 1989.

Vercoutter J. "L'Égypte et la Vallée du Nil, Tome 1: Des Origines à la Fin de l'Ancien Empire." Nouvelle Clio. Presses Universitaires de France. Paris, 1992: p. 30, 33.

Vigoroux Fr. "Dictionnaire de la Bible." Tome Troisième, Premiere Partie. Paris, 1912: p. 337-342.

Virgil. "Georgicon II, 91" in "P. Virgilii Maronis. Bucolica, Georgica et Aeneis." Nicolai Erythraci, Imp. Heirs of Melchiore Sessa. Venice, 1586.

Wilkinson A. "The Garden in Ancient Egypt." The Rubicon Press. London, 1998: p. 104.

Wilson H. "Egyptian Food and Drink." Shire Egyptology. London, 2001: p. 21, 35-43, 47.

"Wörterbuch der Ägyptischen Sprache" (see Erman and Grapow).
    Irp: Wörterbuch I, 1926: p. 115.
    Šdḥ: Wörterbuch IV, 1930: p. 568.

Zugla M. and Kiss A. "Alcaline degradation of parent chromonoid compounds (chromone, flavone, isoflavone)." Acta Chimica Hungarica 124 (1987): 458-489.

www.ingramcontent.com/pod-product-compliance
Lightning Source LLC
Chambersburg PA
CBHW061304270326
41932CB00029B/3466